Three
Quest
Plays

Three Quest Plays

JoAnne James

Red Deer College Press
in association with Players Press/EPS

The Publishers
Red Deer College Press
56 Avenue & 32 Street Box 5005
Red Deer Alberta Canada T4N 5H5
in association with Players Press/EPS
Simultaneously published in Australia, Canada, U.S. and U.K.

Acknowledgments
Edited for the Press by Joyce Doolittle.
Cover art by Scott Barham.
Cover and text design by Dennis Johnson.
Printed and bound in Canada by Parkland ColourPress for Red Deer College Press.

Financial support provided by the Alberta Foundation for the Arts, a beneficiary of the Lottery Fund of the Government of Alberta, and by the Canada Council, the Department of Canadian Heritage and Red Deer College.

COMMITTED TO THE DEVELOPMENT OF CULTURE AND THE ARTS

Canadian Cataloguing in Publication Data
James, JoAnne, 1954–
Three quest plays
ISBN 0-88995-156-X
I. Title.
PS8569.A65T48   1996   C812'.54   C96-910306-9
PR9199.3.J3765T48   1996

Library of Congress Cataloging-in-Publication Data
James, JoAnne.
[Plays. Selections]
Three quest plays / JoAnne James.
    p.   cm.
Contents: The echo box — Moving day — Willa and Sam.
ISBN 0-88734-682-0 (alk. paper)
1. Friendship—Drama. I. Title.
PS3560.A3848A3 1996
812'.54—dc20   96-26703
                                                CIP

For Ryan and Gemma,
who are always in my heart

Contents

The Echo Box

CHARACTERS

Nora

Quiet but full of surprises. An only child accustomed to being an outsider. Although only ten she has already built up a wall of defense by being a smart aleck, using wisecracks to protect herself from being teased by other kids.

Mitchell

The oldest at eleven. A leader at the beach but only because Hallie has always looked up to him. A strong-willed only child, indulged by his parents, he never quite fits in.

Hallie

The youngest at nine. Excitable, a lover of mysteries, drama, danger. Endlessly curious, she loves the outdoors and knows lots about the ocean and its animals.

SCENE ONE: THE ARRIVAL

It is late summer at Saratoga Beach, and the action of the play takes place over about nine days. It opens in the early morning.

There is an old lifeguard's chair that never has a lifeguard in it. The kids climb on it. It's wide enough for only two of them to sit on at once. The dock has three levels and extends out over a round ground cloth depicting the water. There are a picnic table on the dock and a couple of logs on the beach. In the background are broken-down fencing and trees.

All three actors enter through the aisles or the audience, singing. The song suggests arrival at a long-awaited destination. It is performed as an introduction only, with no interaction between the actors during this song.

The song is followed by an introduction to the music that will be heard throughout the play. It is dreamy and playful. It suggests heroes and adventure.

Nora: Land of the silver birch . . .
Mitchell: Home of the beaver . . .
Hallie: Where once the mighty moose wandered at bay . . .
Nora: Blue sky and rocky shore . . .
Hallie: I will return once more . . .
All: Boom da-da boom . . .
Repeat Together: Land of the silver birch
   Home of the beaver
   Where once the mighty moose wandered at bay
   Blue sky and rocky shore
   I will return once more
   Boom da-da boom da . . .
   [NORA and MITCHELL exit.]

SCENE TWO: REUNION

[Music up as HALLIE arrives at the beach with her beach blanket, bag, and sun umbrella.]

Hallie: Alone at last! Perfect!

[Starts spreading out her belongings, taking great care with each object.]

No sister. No nerd-ball brother. Just me. *[Up goes the umbrella.]* And Nature! Exactly what I need for my first picture!

[Takes pieces of driftwood out of her bag, which has the word memoir *decorating it. She is setting the stage for her photo and happily chatters to herself while she works.]*

I'll just move this over a little bit. No . . . much better here. Just about right.

[When she has everything arranged perfectly, she carefully removes her most prized possession from her bag—her camera. Maybe she kisses it before she carefully looks through the lens to check out everything she

has included in her composition.]
Almost perfect. But it still needs something. . . .
[MITCHELL enters and watches HALLIE quietly while slow-ly moving himself into the frame. HALLIE continues look-ing through the viewfinder until she sees him waving at her through the lens.]
Hallie: Mitchell!
Mitchell: Hey! Hallie.
Hallie: Mitchell, Mitchell, Wiener Schnitzel!
Mitchell: How are you doing?
Hallie: When did you get here? I've been coming by your cabin every half hour since we got here yesterday.
Mitchell: Last night. Late.
Hallie: Actually, your timing is just right.
[Before he realizes what HALLIE is doing, MITCHELL has been posed for a photo. She is making a big deal, trying to get him to notice the camera and, at the same time, making him hold the memoir sign and pose. She sits him down on the dock, backs up to look through the lens, then rearranges some of the stuff around him. He dis-covers some cookies in her bag and starts eating them, not paying much attention to what she is doing.]
So . . . how do you like it?
Mitchell: Like what?
Hallie: *[holds up her camera]* What else?
Mitchell: Yeah, where did you—
Hallie: For my birthday.
Mitchell: Neat. When was your—
Hallie: *[whispering, like she is sharing a long-held secret]*
And I used up all my allowance on film for my summer project.
Mitchell: What summer project?
[HALLIE looks in her bag for her hat but finds a big plastic

baggy with two film boxes in it, one of them already open.]

Hallie: See? I have enough film to take forty-eight pictures.
For my book!

Mitchell: You mean like a photo album?

Hallie: *[Her face makes it clear how boring she thinks photo albums are.]* Get a life. No way! This is gonna be . . . a memory book.

[When HALLIE gets no response, she grabs the cookies from him and puts them back into her bag.]

Of the summer! You know what that's called?

Mitchell: No, what?

Hallie: A memoir! I'm going to record everything that happens. *[She finally finds her hat.]* Here, put this on.

Mitchell: What for?

Hallie: For the picture!

[They struggle with the hat as MITCHELL resists putting it on.]

Mitchell: But this looks—

Hallie: Perfect! *[Clicks a picture.]*

Mitchell: But I—

Hallie: Smile! Say *pizza! [Clicks another picture.]*

Mitchell: But I wasn't even—

Hallie: Smile!

Mitchell: —ready! I looked like a dweeb!

Hallie: Perfect. Say *dweeb! [Click. Another picture.]* My title page. The first of forty-eight.

Mitchell: What?

Hallie: It's going to be exactly forty-eight pages long.

Mitchell: Why?

Hallie: Because there are twenty-four pictures in Roll Number One and twenty-four pictures in Roll Number Two.

Mitchell: Sounds like homework! You're going to write forty-eight pages?

Hallie: Later, just like a reporter does. My mom loaned me her tape recorder. I'll show you. *[Looks through her bag for her tape recorder.]*

Mitchell: What are you going to use it for?

Hallie: For talking. All I have to do is talk into it. And talking has never been a problem for me, at least with people I know, right?

Mitchell: That's for sure.

Hallie: Then in the winter, when there's nothing to do— that's when I can write it all down. *[She realizes that her tape recorder is not in her bag after all.]* I must have left it up at the trailer. Come on. Let's go get it so I can interview you.

Mitchell: About what?

Hallie: About . . . how was your winter. About spy theater. *[Starts to run out.]* About swimming, fishing—about that booger you have hangin' off your nose.

Mitchell: What?

Hallie: Come on. I'll race you up the beach.

[MITCHELL and HALLIE exit.]

Scene Three: The Newcomer

[NORA enters the dock carrying her backpack. She puts it down and removes a huge tin of mosquito repellent, a "Safety Around Bears" pamphlet, a flyswatter, a giant can of Raid, and six cans that she has strung together as a noisemaker to frighten bears. She puts these around her neck, then sits down and pulls a jumbo-sized tube of sunscreen from her pack. She begins to slather it all over her legs when she is startled by a noise.]

Nora: What was that? Who's there? I'm not afraid. I'm prepared.

[She pulls out her flyswatter, prepared to use it as a weapon, then swings it wildly around until she actually slaps one onto the log. Looks at the dead bug.]
Oh, gross. . . . See? I'm ready for you. And just on the off chance you're a bear . . . let's get something straight, okay? I'm not here to get between you and any cubs. Got it? Just going to sit here very quietly and look at the water. . . . I'm whale watching, okay?
[She sits still for about thirty seconds, then shakes her six tin cans as loudly as she can. The noise has attracted MITCHELL. He stands off to the side, watching NORA. She has not seen him yet. NORA finally takes out a book but is too restless and nervous to read. Then she notices the camera HALLIE has left behind. Curious, she picks it up to look at it. MITCHELL reacts swiftly.]
Mitchell: Hey! What do you think you're doing?
Nora: Oh! . . . Oh, you scared me.
Mitchell: I said what do you think you're doing?
Nora: I was just—
Mitchell: Put that down.
Nora: I was just looking—
Mitchell: Put it down!
Nora: I will. I'm sorry. *[Puts the camera back exactly where she got it.]*
Mitchell: That's better.
Nora: I was just looking at it.
Mitchell: Well, don't. It's not yours.
Nora: I know that. Is it yours?
Mitchell: No. But it belongs to a friend of mine.
    [At this point, NORA tries to be friendly. She moves to the lifeguard's chair.]
Nora: Your friend must have excellent stuff.
Mitchell: I guess. . . . And that's our chair.

Nora: Oh, sorry.

Mitchell: We were here first. See my initials?

[NORA relocates to the picnic table, leaving her tin cans on the chair and dropping her pamphlet on the way to the table.]

Nora: Sorry, okay? I'll just sit over here.

Mitchell: Fine.

Nora: You don't have to act like the Terminator, you know.

[Pause. They settle into their places. MITCHELL climbs to the top of the chair. Now that he has established his territory, he is willing to open up a bit, but he's not sure how to proceed. He decides that a little friendly teasing would be okay and gets down off the chair.]

Mitchell: Where are you from anyway?

Nora: Just in case it's any of your business.

[MITCHELL picks up tin cans she has strung together.]

Mitchell: What are these for?

Nora: Nothing.

Mitchell: Did you just get married or something?

Nora: Very funny.

Mitchell: They sort of remind me of something. *[Puts the tin cans around his neck.]*

Nora: What?

Mitchell: When we used to go camping up at Banff, my grandma used to carry something like this.

[NORA ignores him.]

She used to carry it with her whenever she went off to the outhouse. You know why?

Nora: No.

Mitchell: To scare away the bears, that's why!

Nora: Good for her.

Mitchell: That's what you're doing with this, isn't it?

Nora: No, I—

Mitchell: You're going to run all over the beach shaking these cans, right?

Nora: No, it's a . . . it's a . . .

Mitchell: A what?

Nora: It's a craft project, that's what.

Mitchell: A craft project?

[NORA has to think fast to make this up.]

Nora: Yeah. I'm going to look for sand dollars and string them on here. To make Christmas decorations.

Mitchell: Really?

Nora: Really. It's a present for my mother.

[While NORA is busy trying to ignore him, MITCHELL picks up the pamphlet she has dropped. He holds it up and we see the title: "Safety Around Bears."]

Mitchell: Then what's this?

Nora: Give that back.

Mitchell: Yoo-hoo. . . . Bears!

[NORA chases him, trying to retrieve her pamphlet.]

Calling all grizzly bears!

Nora: Give it back!

[Chase continues.]

Mitchell: You bears better not mess with me! I've got these cans!

Nora: Give it back. It's mine!

[Chase continues.]

Mitchell: Didn't anybody tell you that there are no grizzlies on Vancouver Island?

Nora: No.

Mitchell: Not unless they take the ferry across!

[NORA gives up on the chase and starts picking up some shells to look at. She tries to ignore MITCHELL.]

Nora: Very funny.

Mitchell: Is it your first time at Saratoga Beach or what?

Nora: Yeah . . . and I hope it's my last.

Mitchell: Why?

Nora: There's nothing to do.

Mitchell: Yes there is.

Nora: Like what? There's no TV, no video games . . . and every mosquito on Planet Earth lives here!

Mitchell: They do not! Have you ever been to Winnipeg?

Nora: They do so. I already have three bites on this arm. And I have about ten on each leg.

Mitchell: Why did you come here then?

Nora: My mother made me, that's why.

Mitchell: Well, if you hate it so much, why don't you just . . .

Nora: Just what?

[Before he leaves, MITCHELL throws the string of cans and the pamphlet at her.]

Mitchell: Just leave! *[roaring like a bear]* Go back to where you came from!

[NORA, rattled, drops her bag. MITCHELL laughs as he exits. Music up.]

SCENE FOUR: MAKING FRIENDS

[NORA is reading a Nancy Drew mystery at the picnic table when HALLIE enters.]

Hallie: Mitchell, Mitchell, Wiener Schnitzel? Are you out here?

Nora: Was he wearing a green T-shirt?

Hallie: Yeah, he was.

Nora: The Terminator? He went that way.

Hallie: The what?

Nora: Never mind.

[Pause. HALLIE crosses over to her stuff, dries off with her beach towel, and puts on some sunscreen. She checks NORA out the whole time.]

What's wrong? Am I on your spot or something?

Hallie: Just looking at your book, that's all. I read that one.

Nora: You did?

Hallie: *The Mystery of Miner's Creek.* Scary, right?

Nora: Yeah, I guess.

Hallie: Yeah. Especially the search chapter. When Nancy goes to the abandoned mine. . . .

Nora: The abandoned mine?

[HALLIE moves behind the lifeguard's chair and climbs through the back as if the underside is the mine shaft in the ghost town.]

Hallie: And that guy takes out the dynamite?

Nora: What?

Hallie: And it's so creepy-crawly, and then—

Nora: Hey, wait a minute. I'm not there yet!

Hallie: Oh. Sorry! It's the best part. Well, you'll like it.

[Pause. HALLIE climbs up to the chair's seat with her towel and cookies.]

Nora: Does she fall in?

Hallie: No way. You know Nancy Drew. She gets to be the hero! The rescue is . . . Well, I don't want to wreck it for you. *[Makes herself comfortable in her seat, then starts in on her cookies.]* Want one?

Nora: Okay. *[On her way up, she plays at making a big dramatic fall.]* At least I know she doesn't . . . fall in! *[They both laugh. NORA reaches the top and sits beside HALLIE. They look around for a moment, each with a cookie. Pause.]*

Hallie: Don't you just love Nancy Drew. She's just so . . .

Nora: Brave.

Hallie: Strong.

Nora: Loyal. I like how she's such a good friend.

Hallie: To Bess and George, right? Like, she gets them out of trouble. Even when they do something stupid.

Nora: Remember that time they all got locked in?

Hallie: In the basement of the old mill?

Nora: That was in one of my favorites. *The Search for Cindy Austin.*

Hallie: Mine, too.

Nora: Nancy Drew can do anything, right?

Hallie: Swim across rivers . . .

Nora: Jump out of burning buildings . . .

Hallie: Ride horses . . .

[They begin to slowly ride imaginary horses together as they sit on top of the chair. They ride through the next few lines.]

Nora: To the rescue!

Hallie: To the rescue!

Nora: She's my hero!

Hallie: Mine, too!

[They grin at each other, unsure what to do next. They share that exquisite and almost unbearable excitement that young girls feel when they make a new friend.] Never even saw you before.

Nora: I know.

Hallie: Why don't you tell me what your name is? So I don't have to call you Whatever Your Name Is!

Nora: It's Nora.

Hallie: I'm Hallie.

Nora: Never heard that name before.

Hallie: Nobody has. *[Takes her time, slowly deciding to confide.]* You won't believe what it's short for.

Nora: What?

Hallie: You'll laugh.

Nora: Won't. I promise.

Hallie: Haliburton. My mom named me after her hometown. It's in Nova Scotia.

[NORA can't help giggling. Neither can HALLIE.]

Nora: Really? She named you after a town? Is that where you're from?

Hallie: No, we're from Edmonton. But my mom grew up there. In Haliburton, I mean.

Nora: Oh. Well, Hallie's okay. I like it.

Hallie: Thanks.

Nora: Could be *a lot* worse. She could be from . . . Medicine Hat!

Hallie: Or Chicoutimi!

Nora: She could have called you Rainbow. Or Moonbeam. I knew a kid named Tree once.

[They both laugh, surprised to have had so much fun together already. The next few lines are spoken on top of each other as the girls' excitement at making a new friend overcomes any shyness.]

Hallie: So is this your first time at the beach?

Nora: Is your whole family here?

Both: Where are you staying?

Hallie: Jinx!

Nora: Do you ever get bored here?

Hallie: Bored? Here? No way. There's so much to do.

Nora: Like what?

[HALLIE climbs down from the chair and goes to the end of the dock to swing on the ladder arms. NORA follows suit.]

Hallie: Well, we swim every day. And we paddle around in a little boat.

Nora: Is it yours?

Hallie: Mine and my nerd-ball brother's. I can take you out for a ride in it later if you like.

Nora: Okay.

Hallie: Do you like hot dogs?

Nora: Sure.

Hallie: Good, because at night we have bonfires.

Nora: Really?

Hallie: Every night. We roast hot dogs and marshmallows. And see those logs up there?

Nora: Yeah.

Hallie: Last year, that's where we built the biggest sand castle you ever saw. With moats and—

Nora: And bridges?

Hallie: And everything. We used these huge shovels, right? *[Builds an imaginary castle.]* Spent the whole morning on it. Then, in the afternoon, we sat and watched it just . . . whoosh!

Nora: Whoosh!

Hallie: Got swept away by the tide. Till there was nothing left. Not even the secret passage.
[They kneel on the beach for a moment. HALLIE picks up some shells to show NORA, then jumps up as she thinks of something else.]
Hey, have you ever played Sardines? You know, where it's like tag? *[She tags NORA to demonstrate.]* Only every time you get caught, you just all stick together? *[Sticks herself to NORA, and they play at this for a bit.]* It's more fun with lots of kids, isn't it?

Nora: Yeah.

Hallie: You played stuff like this back home, right?

Nora: Oh, sure. Me and my friends? We have lots of games like that. Me and my friends.

Hallie: Well, Mitchell and I play Spy Theater. All around here on the beach. And up there on the campground.

Nora: Spy Theater?

Hallie: Yeah. It's the best. Maybe you'd like—

Nora: *[eagerly]* To what?

Hallie: To play it with us. Tomorrow.

Nora: Sure, I'd love to.

[Pause.]

Do you come here every year?

Hallie: Yeah. For two weeks every summer. My mom says watching the tides slows us down. Makes us appreciate things more. My mom's always trying to get me to slow down.

Nora: Looks pretty slow to me.

Hallie: You'll see. It's magic here. Can you feel it?

Nora: Sort of.

Hallie: Hey, wait a minute. . . .

Nora: What?

[HALLIE gets out her tape recorder, climbs on the picnic table, and takes a photo of NORA.]

Hallie: You have to go into my memoir!

Nora: Your what?

Hallie: My memory book of the summer! I'll record what you say, and then I'll write it down later. Testing, testing . . . *[pushing the microphone toward her]* So your name's Nora. Where are you from?

Nora: Calgary.

Hallie: Where are you staying? Campground or one of the cabins?

Nora: Cabin 2.

Hallie: Is your whole family here?

Nora: No, just me. And my aunt and uncle.

Hallie: What's the best thing about the cabin?

Nora: Sleeping in a bunk bed.

Hallie: What's the worst?

Nora: The outhouse!

Hallie: Oh, yeah!

Nora: Once, when I was little, my mom took me camping, and I looked down there and I knew there was trouble. I didn't have too many words yet, but I came running back to the cabin saying, "Danger! Danger!" Now it's a big joke in my family, and every time somebody has to go, we tease them and say, "Danger! Danger!"

Hallie: Danger! Danger! But how do you like it here? So far, I mean?

Nora: It's getting better. Have to go now, though.

Hallie: Oh. Okay.

Nora: Told my aunt I wouldn't be long. See you tomorrow.

Hallie: Bye.

[The look they exchange acknowledges the importance of the last few minutes. NORA exits. HALLIE carries the tape recorder up to the chair. She looks out at the water.]

I was remembering what it was like here last year. Especially after supper. One night, there was a shooting star, and my whole family lay down on the beach waiting for another one. It never came.

[Music up.]

But, you know? It was one of our best times of the summer—everybody flat on their backs, quiet, watching the sky. Expecting something . . . magic, holding our breaths. Just being together, waiting. You had this feeling, you know? That anything could happen.

[Music. HALLIE exits.]

SCENE FIVE: SPY THEATER

[Music up. Early evening. NORA is waiting on the dock as MITCHELL and HALLIE approach. HALLIE is wearing her camera on a strap around her neck and stripes of brightly colored zinc ointment on her nose and across her cheeks. She has stopped to paint the same stripes on MITCHELL. The first few lines take place out of NORA's earshot.]

Mitchell: Don't look now, but there's someone on our dock.

Hallie: What are you talking . . .

> [MITCHELL *holds up a felt marker, pretending it's a spray gun.*]

Mitchell: Good thing I brought my SSFP.

Hallie: Your what?

Mitchell: My Super Sonic Flea Powder! To get rid of unwanted pests.

Hallie: *[shoves MITCHELL]* Don't be such a dweeb.

> [HALLIE *heads up to the dock to welcome NORA. Pulls her by the hand.*]

Hallie: Great, you're here. Did you two meet yet?

Nora: Well, I . . .

Hallie: Nora, this is Mitchell.

> [HALLIE *waits for them to acknowledge each other. They don't.*]

Well? Aren't you going to say hello?

Mitchell: We've already met.

Nora: Sort of.

Hallie: Perfect.

> [HALLIE *looks at them. She decides they are just being shy.*]

Did you two realize that you already have two things in common?

Mitchell: Like what?

Hallie: Well, first, you're both friends with me, right?

> [NORA *rolls her eyeballs.* MITCHELL *puts his finger down his throat.*]

Hallie: And, second, you're both from Calgary.

Both: What?

> [MITCHELL *and* HALLIE *look at each other in complete horror.* HALLIE *brings the pile of stuff for Spy Theater—sunglasses, hats, and so on—upstage to sort it into three piles.* MITCHELL *calls over to her.*]

Mitchell: Calgary's a big city, Hallie. It's not like we're neighbors or anything, right?

Nora: Right.

Mitchell: At least, I hope not. What part of Calgary are you from?

Nora: Sunnyside.

Mitchell: Good. I'm from Bowness.

[HALLIE crosses to get something else.]

Hallie: Are they close together?

Both: No.

Nora: Thank goodness.

Mitchell: Bowness used to be its own town. Did you know that?

Nora: No.

Mitchell: It used to be *all* on its own, completely independent. Its own main street, its own mayor, everything. Completely different from Calgary.

Nora: Big hairy deal.

Mitchell: And we have Bowness Park. It's only the biggest park in Calgary.

Nora: And we have Riley Park. And Prince's Island Park.

Mitchell: We have Canada Olympic Park.

Nora: And we're right beside the zoo. Maybe you've been there?

Mitchell: Of course I have.

Nora: Visiting your gorilla friends, I bet!

[HALLIE returns and starts painting NORA's face with zinc ointment.]

Nora: What is this stuff?

Hallie: It's for Spy Theater. Mitchell, did you explain the rules to her?

Mitchell: What?

Hallie: Nora's going to play with us.

Mitchell: But that's our game.

Hallie: I know.

Mitchell: We made it up.

Hallie: It'll be way more fun with three.

Mitchell: *[to HALLIE]* But she's weird!

Hallie: She is not.

Mitchell: She is so. She's one of the people I wanted to spy on!

Hallie: You're the one who's being weird.

Mitchell: But she's a geek. . . . Can't you see that?

Nora: *[ignoring MITCHELL]* What do we do?

Hallie: Well, first we take these flashlights. And we wear these neon stripes on our faces.

> *[MITCHELL sees his next chance to get rid of NORA . He'll scare her away. He starts to circle her. HALLIE joins in cheerfully, seeing this simply as a fun way to explain the game to NORA.]*

Mitchell: So we can glow in the dark and help scare away some of the sand snakes.

Hallie: And we go to the campground and the cabins.

Mitchell: Watching out for *bears* of course.

Hallie: Sneaking along as quietly as we can.

Mitchell: We're not afraid of anything. Not mosquitoes.

Hallie: Not the dark.

Mitchell: Not sharks.

Hallie: And we sneak into people's campsites very quietly.

Mitchell: And spy on them.

Hallie: *[stops circling]* And then we make up stories about them. We turn this chair into a theater. *[drapes her beach towel over the top of the chair]* We make a curtain, and then we act out the stories. See?

Nora: Not really.

Hallie: Sometimes we get all the families to watch. Most times, it's just the little kids.

Nora: I don't really get it.

Mitchell: Do we have to draw a picture?

Hallie: It's like this—we'll show you. Last year, there was a lady in Cabin 4 who was just like an acrobat. Remember, Mitchell?

Mitchell: Yep.

Hallie: Every morning, she used to get up really early and do all these, like, contortions on her deck.

[HALLIE tries to demonstrate a difficult pose but falls down laughing. MITCHELL joins her attempt to demonstrate. He thinks that if they really show off, it will get rid of NORA.]

Mitchell: She looked like an alien!

Hallie: But she sort of reminded us of an acrobat. So we made up this story about a family of circus acrobats who came camping, right?

[They do some tumbling, including handstands. MITCHELL walks around on his hands.]

See the swing set up there? We got my dad to shorten the ropes into a trapeze.

Mitchell: You have to be really coordinated to do this, you know. Else you might break your neck.

Hallie: Yeah.

Mitchell: Remember when we tried to do the human pyramid?

Hallie: With the little kids?

Mitchell: Splat, right?

Hallie: We went up and asked everyone in the campground for their tarps. And we made this whole place into a circus tent. It was great, wasn't it?

Mitchell: The best.

Hallie: When we were taking admission, we played we were monkeys.

Mitchell: Yep. Maybe we can be bears this time. *[He growls at NORA.]*

Hallie: Spy Theater is my favorite. We've been playing it every summer since we were four.

Mitchell: By ourselves.

Hallie: It's fun!

[MITCHELL pulls HALLIE aside.]

Mitchell: But it's our game.

Hallie: It'll be even more fun with three.

Mitchell: But there are only two routes.

Nora: We could still have two routes. I could go with Hallie.

Hallie: Exactly! We'll be partners.

[HALLIE puts the finishing touches on NORA's face and takes a picture.]

Mitchell: But I only brought enough stuff for two.

Hallie: I brought everything she needs. There! Doesn't she look just like us?

Mitchell: Not quite.

Hallie: We'll meet you back here in ten minutes, okay?

Mitchell: Okay, okay.

[HALLIE and NORA leave. Music up. Alone, MITCHELL does one more headstand, then exits.]

SCENE SIX: NANCY DREW

[NORA tiptoes back in, giggling. HALLIE follows. Both are whispering.]

Hallie: Is the coast clear?

Nora: Looks like it.

Hallie: Think we were followed?

Nora: Not sure. *[She checks around carefully.]*

Hallie: Nora? Let's put clues over at the boat launch.

Nora: We can put clues anywhere we want to, *Bess*. And don't call me Nora.

Hallie: Sorry, I forgot . . .

[HALLIE takes out her tape recorder, speaks into the mike.]
. . . that you're Everybody's Favorite Hero . . .

Nora: Nancy Drew! The world's youngest and most brilliant detective.

Hallie: Accompanied by your trusted friend Bess, who, at this very moment, is helping Nancy to establish . . .

Nora: Headquarters at Saratoga Beach. Remember that in order to solve the case, no one can hear our plans.

[As HALLIE snaps a photo of NORA, MITCHELL enters with a Spy Theater idea that he is sure will frighten NORA off. He interrupts them.]

Mitchell: Hey, did you see the new family with the jeep? They've got a boa constrictor in a cage. . . .

Nora: Stop right there!

Mitchell: What?

Hallie: Security headquarters, you know.

Nora: We have to be very careful.

Mitchell: About what?

Nora: About intruders, that's what. We are trying to solve a very important case here.

[HALLIE looks around to be sure she will not be overheard.]

Hallie: The Case of the Missing Canoe.

Mitchell: What canoe?

Hallie: Up at Cabin 1? There was a canoe there this morning.

Nora: And now it's disappeared!

Mitchell: So what? They probably took it out. Boats *belong* in the water you know, Einstein.

Nora: Oh, you're so smart.

Mitchell: Wait a minute. What about Spy Theater?

[HALLIE and NORA start to climb up the lifeguard's chair, leaving MITCHELL below.]

Hallie: We were going to but then . . . we were talking about our heroes, and Nora had this great idea. . . .

Mitchell: About what?

Hallie: About playing our heroes.

Nora: Heroes to the rescue!

Hallie: Every day we'll do a different hero.

Nora: Like Nancy Drew!

Hallie: Like She-Ra, Princess of Power!

Nora: Like Catwoman!

Hallie: Like—

Mitchell: Wait a minute. There are lots of other heroes.

Nora: Like who?

Mitchell: What about Robin Hood? Batman? Or Indiana Jones?

[NORA and HALLIE immediately launch into theme music from Indiana Jones *and leap from the lifeguard's chair to the dock.]*

Hallie: Perfect! We can play all the heroes. All summer! But let's start with Nancy Drew. . . .

Nora: We're gonna do a robbery mystery. About what happened to that canoe.

Hallie: And she's gonna to be Nancy Drew.

Mitchell: Oh, right.

Hallie: And we'll take turns making up mysteries. And we'll leave clues all over the beach.

Mitchell: But what about *Spy Theater?*

Nora: It's stupid.

Mitchell: What do you mean?

Nora: Who wants to make up sucky stories about monkeys playing circus on the beach?

Hallie: We'll still play Spy Theater, but let's do this first.

Nora: It's a baby game. You said you've been playing it since you were four.

Mitchell: So?

Hallie: So maybe it's time for a new game. That's all she means.

Nora: Okay, look. Have you read any Nancy Drew books?

Mitchell: No.

Nora: Oh, brother. Do I have to draw a picture?

Hallie: He's read the Hardy Boys though, right, Mitch?

Mitchell: Yeah.

Hallie: Well, it's sort of like that.

Nora: Only better! Because it's all girls! And everyone knows girls are smarter!

Hallie: Faster!

Nora: Stronger!

Mitchell: Very funny.

Hallie: Okay, look. Nancy has two friends. One is Bess. That's me. And the other one's George . . .

Nora: Who's a *girl*.

Hallie: Which makes it perfect. We don't even have to change the name.

Nora: But I . . .

Hallie: Just explain the rest to him.

Nora: Do I have to?

Hallie: Come on, you guys. I'll go get us some Popsicles, okay? *[HALLIE exits. When HALLIE leaves, NORA sees her chance to get rid of MITCHELL. When he tries to climb the lifeguard's chair during the next few lines, she does not let him.]*

Mitchell: Okay, how do you play?

Nora: Well, I'm the hero.

Mitchell: Of course.

Nora: And you just do everything I say.

Mitchell: Oh, sure.

Nora: That's the rule. Because I'm Nancy Drew.

Mitchell: Big hairy deal.

Nora: That means I'm in charge. Got it?

Mitchell: What do you mean?

Nora: I decide what you have to do. I might decide that you can't play with Hallie.

Mitchell: Hallie's my friend.

Nora: She's mine, too.

Mitchell: She was my friend first.

Nora: So? She your girlfriend? Do you go under the dock and kiss or what?

Mitchell: No way.

Nora: Well, I'm in charge now. You have to follow my orders. . . .

Mitchell: What if I don't want to?

Nora: Then don't. I'm sure you could find some little kids to play with.

[Pause. They glare at each other.]

Nora: Mitchell, Mitchell. . . .

Mitchell: Shut up.

Nora: Mitchell, Mitchell, Wiener Schnitzel.

Mitchell: Just shut up.

Nora: Mitchell, Mitchell, Wiener Schnitzel.

Mitchell: I don't even want to play your stupid game.

Nora: Good. Why don't you go play one of your baby games?

Mitchell: Leave me alone.

Nora: Okay. I'll go find Hallie. Maybe you can find some four-year-olds to play with.

[Nora runs out. Music up. Mitchell exits slowly in the other direction.]

SCENE SEVEN: TABLEAUX

[This brief scene shows us the passage of several days. It is composed of scenes from the girls' mystery games,

which are being captured for HALLIE's summer memoir. It is played as if the audience is flipping through the memoir and seeing each photo as it is being taken. Each setup is quick, music is upbeat, and action is fast and may be improvised, except for one ritual moment each time when HALLIE carefully records the date and name of that day's mystery.

Enter HALLIE carrying her camera. NORA follows with a paddle and a bucket of seaweed. NORA is wearing a bathing cap.]

Hallie: Okay, hold it right there. No hold the paddle closer to your side. And don't forget the seaweed. That was the clue. Okay, here goes. Tuesday, August 16: The Case of the Missing Rowboat. Perfect!

[Music up. They dump the stuff on the picnic table and exit. Time passes. MITCHELL enters and watches from the sidelines without being seen. HALLIE and NORA enter carrying a picnic basket.]

Would you stop eating the sandwiches? How am I supposed to get this? Okay, put down the thermos. Hold up the glass of Kool-Aid. Here goes. Wednesday, August 17: The Case of the Moonlit Picnic. Perfect!

[The girls leave their stuff on the picnic table and exit. Music up. Time passes. MITCHELL watches again from another place. He is very clearly excluded. Music up. Time passes.

NORA runs in and climbs up to the lifeguard's chair, then hangs upside down. Again MITCHELL watches without being seen.]

Nora: Hallie! Help! Hallie!

[HALLIE runs in without even noticing MITCHELL. He sulks away.]

Hallie: Nora! Are you okay?

Nora: It's for the picture!

Hallie: Oh, perfect. Thursday August 18: The Case of the Twisted Corpse.

Nora: Hurry up and take it before I hurl.

Hallie: Can you look a little more twisted? There!

Nora: Help! I'm stuck!

[HALLIE helps her down, and they run off with most of their stuff. HALLIE's arms are full, so she leaves the camera behind on the dock.]

SCENE 8: THE BROKEN CAMERA

[The camera and tape recorder have been left behind. MITCHELL approaches the picnic table and kicks a bucket they have left behind. He removes the mike from the tape recorder and fools around with it but does not record anything.]

Mitchell: Got a case for you, Hallie. How about The Case of The Creepy Crawler from Cabin 2? Your friend Nora? She's a butt-head! Ever since she got here, this place has started to suck. All you do every single day is play Nancy Drew. And in every case, it's Nora who gets to be the hero.

[MITCHELL picks up the camera and starts twirling it.]

Ever notice that? That you never get to be Nancy Drew? All you ever get to do is worship her and bring her Popsicles.

[MITCHELL takes the camera and starts twirling it by its strap, taking big bows as if he's being presented to the Queen.]

Oh, Nancy, you are so smart. You are the bravest detective in the world. You are my hero. . . .

[As MITCHELL swings around, he accidentally swings the camera into the side of the lifeguard's chair. The back

of the camera breaks. The film pops out and hangs from the back. He carries it to the dock and tries to put it back together, then looks around to make sure no one has seen him. He runs out, shoving the tape recorder into his jacket pocket. The broken camera is left behind, lying on the dock.

Music up.

NORA enters, carrying a small paper bag. She immediately notices the camera and picks it up. As she examines it, HALLIE enters.]

Hallie: Nora? Listen, I've got a great idea for . . . *[sees the camera]* What happened?

Nora: I don't know. I . . .

Hallie: What did you do?

Nora: I didn't . . .

Hallie: The back won't shut.

Nora: Let me see. *[trying to take it back]*

[MITCHELL has overheard them and come back. He listens quietly for a minute before they notice him.]

Hallie: My camera.

Nora: Maybe we can fix it.

Hallie: The film's all hanging out.

Nora: Can't we just put it back?

Hallie: No we can't. All my summer pictures are gonna be wrecked.

Nora: Well, maybe we could . . .

Hallie: My memory book. I won't be able to . . .

Nora: Hallie, I . . . *[reaches for the camera]*

Hallie: Don't touch it.

Nora: But I just want to help.

Hallie: Get your hands off it.

Nora: But Hallie.

Hallie: What did you do?

[Pause. MITCHELL sees his opportunity and moves forward.]

Mitchell: She broke it. That's what she did.

Nora: I did not.

Mitchell: She did so, Hallie. And she threw your tape recorder over there.

Hallie: How do you know?

Mitchell: Because I saw her do it.

Nora: You never did!

Mitchell: I saw the whole thing, Hallie.

Nora: It was broken when I got here. I never even touched it before.

Hallie: And where's my tape recorder?

Nora: I don't know.

Mitchell: You always keep them together, right?

Hallie: Yes, I do.

Mitchell: The first time I saw her, she was poking around your stuff, Hallie. Did you know that?

Hallie: No.

Mitchell: On the very first day she got here, I had to yell at her and tell her to leave it alone.

Hallie: Is that true?

Nora: Well, yes, but . . .

Hallie: Is it true or not?

Nora: Yes. But I was just looking at it.

Hallie: That's why you called him the Terminator, isn't it? Because he was looking after my stuff.

Mitchell: I guess you were always pretty jealous of it, weren't you, Nancy Drew?

Nora: No . . . I . . .

Mitchell: You even said she had excellent stuff.

Nora: Hallie, listen to me.

Mitchell: Better check her bag, see if she's stealing anything.

[HALLIE grabs NORA's paper bag. Looks inside.]

Nora: It's just my shells. Hallie, listen to me.

Mitchell: Liar, liar, pants on fire . . .

Nora: But I didn't do anything.

Mitchell: Hang you from the telephone wire . . .

Nora: Hallie, please . . . I didn't . . .

[HALLIE hesitates, looking from MITCHELL to NORA.]

Mitchell: Liar, liar, pants on fire. Hang you from the telephone wire.

[HALLIE slowly joins in.]

Mitchell and Hallie: Liar, liar, pants on fire. Hang you from the telephone wire.

Nora: I thought you were my friend.

Mitchell: Come on, Hallie. If we go back there onto the beach, we might be able to find your other stuff.

Hallie: What about the tape recorder? My mom's gonna kill me.

[HALLIE and MITCHELL run out.]

Nora: But I was just looking at it.

[NORA slowly picks up her things and leaves.]

SCENE NINE: JUST LIKE IT USED TO BE

[Music up. It's early morning, five days later. HALLIE is alone on the beach. Silence. MITCHELL tiptoes in with a bucket, goes right to the beach. HALLIE follows slowly, carrying her tape recorder.]

Mitchell: Come on. I know this'll work. You just stand here.

Hallie: Okay, but . . .

[Pause.]

Mitchell: I'll get them into this bucket. I'll corral them.

Hallie: But they don't make any . . .

[Pause.]

Mitchell: It'll make a great recording. Shhhhh . . .

[Pause.]

Hallie: This is dumb!

Mitchell: Shhhhh!

Hallie: Forget it! They don't make any noise! They're minnows!

[HALLIE leaves and climbs the first rungs of the lifeguard's chair.]

Mitchell: I guess you're right. *[follows her over to the lifeguard's chair]* Hey, did you hear the Arctic loons this morning?

Hallie: No. Were they here?

Mitchell: Yeah. My dad saw them when he was jogging. *[Waits for her response. Nothing.]*

We should start practicing our calls.

[MITCHELL starts some calls. HALLIE does not join in.]

Remember the first time I taught you how to do the heron stand? And how to call?

[They both try some loon calls and start to laugh.]

We could come down early tomorrow when the tide is out and stand. See if we can get them to come to our beach.

Hallie: Guess so.

[HALLIE climbs to the top of the chair. MITCHELL hands her up the end of a beach towel to make a curtain.]

Mitchell: Hey, you know those people who just arrived in the silver trailer?

Hallie: Yeah.

Mitchell: I was watching them unload. They've got enough gear to stay here all summer.

Hallie: Good for them.

Mitchell: They sort of remind me of a team or something. We could do them as a football team. Or an army!

Hallie: What?

Mitchell: Spy Theater, remember?

[HALLIE is looking far down the beach.]

Hallie: Oh, yeah. Is that your dad up there with your kite?

[MITCHELL climbs up to the top.]

Mitchell: That's him all right. What's he doing?

Hallie: Looks like he's having trouble.

Mitchell: He's getting it all tangled up again. Sometimes I just wish he'd leave my stuff alone.

Hallie: I know what you mean.

Mitchell: Look at that! I showed him how to rewind it twice already. *[calling]* Dad? Dad! That's not the way it's supposed to go. Wait for me. I'll show you again!

[HALLIE leaves her tape recorder running and begins to talk into it. At the beginning of the speech, she stands on the top of the lifeguard's chair to watch MITCHELL run off down the beach. During the speech, she slowly climbs down to the sand. By the end of it, she is standing at the end of the dock looking out over the water.]

Hallie: That's Mitchell, all right. Wants to play Spy Theater, like we can just go back. But after my camera got broken . . . the whole summer changed after that. I dunno. It's like a big cloud has come over the beach. Every day's been sunny, but it just feels dark somehow.

Yesterday we built a clubhouse under one of the decks. Made a secret entrance with a sleeping bag. It was fun until we discovered a wasps' nest under there.

I'm glad the loons are back. *[tries a loon call]* Wonder if they get homesick. When they call, they always sound so lonely, as if they didn't have a friend in the world.

Mitchell taught me to stand really still, like the herons do when the tide is out. And we'd call them.

[HALLIE turns off the tape recorder, sits quietly for a moment, then tries another loon call.

From behind, unseen by HALLIE, NORA enters and repeats the call, which sounds like an echo. At first, HALLIE thinks it is one of the birds she has been waiting to see all summer. She rises, trying to stand quietly in the heron stand, one leg raised, watching for them. When she realizes that the sound is coming from behind her, she turns. The moment of reverie is broken when she sees NORA standing there.
They look at each other, but HALLIE runs out before NORA can say a word.
Music up.]

SCENE TEN: NORA'S APOLOGY

[NORA alone on dock. Takes the echo box, which is wrapped in newsprint, out of her backpack and holds it. Tries a couple of loon calls. MITCHELL enters on his way back to the cabin with his kite, which is tangled up in a big mess.]

Mitchell: Was that supposed to be a loon call?

Nora: No, I was just . . .

Mitchell: Because you know what? Keep that up and you'll scare all the loons away. *[continues on his way, heading off the beach]*

Nora: Mitchell? Can you wait a minute?

Mitchell: I'm in a hurry.

Nora: But I just . . .

[She tries to grab his arm. He drops the holder of string he has carefully been wrapping back up for his kite. He's annoyed.]

Mitchell: Now look what you made me do.

Nora: Sorry. But I was—

Mitchell: Just leave it. You're making it worse.

[NORA backs off, but not very far.]

Nora: Well, don't worry. You won't need your super sonic flea powder anymore.

Mitchell: Why not?

Nora: Because I'm leaving tomorrow.

Mitchell: Good!

Nora: Mitchell . . . Mitchell, remember how I teased you before? About Spy Theater?

Mitchell: Yeah.

Nora: Before I go . . . I just wanted . . .

[She tries to help him with the string, but he pushes her away.]

Mitchell: Get your hands off it.

Nora: I just wanted to say that . . . I know what it's like to be . . .

Mitchell: To be what?

Nora: To be the one who gets picked on.

Mitchell: You? But I thought you were always in charge.

Nora: No. I just didn't . . .

Mitchell: Didn't what?

Nora: Didn't wanna be left out. Know what I mean?

Mitchell: Not really. Don't care either.

Nora: It's just that it's been a long time since . . .

Mitchell: Since what?

Nora: Since I made a friend like Hallie.

Mitchell: Thought you said you had tons of friends back home.

Nora: No.

Mitchell: Thought there must be hundreds of girls who'd want to play with Nancy Drew.

Nora: Never played it before.

Mitchell: But you looked like such an expert.

[He drops the ball of tangled string. Nora picks it up.]

Nora: I know. But out here, it's different. You can be anyone you want to be . . . out here.

[For the rest of the scene, she helps him sort out the string and roll it up.]

Back home, it's harder. For me, anyway.

Mitchell: Why?

Nora: We just moved again. In June.

Mitchell: So what?

Nora: For the fifth time in two years.

Mitchell: But I thought you were like some big expert on Sunnyside.

[MITCHELL has the kite string rewound. He takes it to the picnic table to put it back in its case. NORA follows.]

Nora: I made that up. And the part about having lots of friends, too. So you were right.

Mitchell: About what?

Nora: About "liar, liar, pants on fire," right?

Mitchell: Guess so.

Nora: And I know what it's like to be teased like that. Just wanted to say I'm sorry.

[MITCHELL has his kite all wrapped up. He doesn't know how to accept the apology. He finds it easier to change the subject.]

Mitchell: So you're leaving?

Nora: Yeah.

Mitchell: Thought you were here for two weeks.

Nora: I phoned my mom. Told her I hate it here.

Mitchell: Because of the mosquitoes, right?

Nora: Yeah.

[MITCHELL stands there awkwardly, not sure what to say. He notices the box.]

Mitchell: What's that?

Nora: Just a present I made.

Mitchell: Is it for your mom?

Nora: No.

Mitchell: Who's it for?

Nora: For Hallie.

Mitchell: Why? It's not her birthday or anything.

Nora: I know. Will you give it to her for me?

[MITCHELL hesitates, almost does it, then decides against it.]

Mitchell: I can't. . . . My . . . uh . . . dad's waiting for me. Gotta go.

[MITCHELL exits.]

SCENE ELEVEN: THE ECHO BOX

[NORA is sitting on the picnic table. Music up as she holds her backpack quietly and looks out at the water. HALLIE enters. When she sees NORA, she tries to leave without being seen. NORA notices her right away and calls out.]

Hallie: Just looking for Mitchell. Have you seen him?

Nora: He just left. To meet his dad.

[HALLIE starts to leave, but NORA stops her.]

Nora: Can you wait just a minute?

Hallie: What for?

Nora: I have something for you. *[opens her backpack and takes out the echo box]*

Hallie: There's only one thing you could give me that I want.

Nora: Hallie . . .

Hallie: A new camera. That's what. Is that what you've got?

Nora: No.

Hallie: *[climbing up onto the chair]* Then I don't want it.

Nora: But I think you'll like this.

[NORA crosses and hands her gift up to HALLIE. It's wrapped in newspaper. As HALLIE unwraps it over the next few lines, we see a box that has been carefully cov-

ered with material, then glued with shells. It is shiny, a little treasure box.]

Hallie: What is it?

Nora: The camera was so you could make a memory book of the summer, right?

Hallie: You know it was.

[NORA is determined to see HALLIE's response to her gift. She climbs up to sit beside her on the chair. HALLIE is just curious enough to stay there and see what it is.]

Nora: Well, I thought you could have a box instead.

Hallie: For what?

Nora: For your memories. It's an echo box. You know those shells, the ones that echo?

Hallie: Yeah.

Nora: I know they're your favorites. So I put some here on top. You could keep your collection in here. And you could keep some of your drawings in here. And some souvenirs from Spy Theater.

[HALLIE can't resist opening the box.]

See? I already put in a couple of things for you.

Hallie: What is all this stuff?

Nora: Well, here's an official postcard.

Hallie: Of Saratoga Beach!

Nora: See? It's even got a heron on it.

Hallie: Did you really make this?

Nora: *[nodding]* My aunt thought I might feel better if I could give you something before I left. And it gave me something to do.

[Pause.]

At first, I couldn't think of anything. But then I figured that if you had a special box, it could hold some souvenirs of the summer. Sort of like a memoir.

[HALLIE examines the box, unsure what to say. NORA

waits for a comment that does not come, then continues nervously. Her pride in the beauty of the box is evident.] So I collected all these baby clam shells. And I glued them on as close together as I could. There are a couple of empty spots.

Hallie: It's beautiful. Feels so smooth.

Nora: That's because I painted over the whole thing with this clear nail polish. My aunt let me borrow it. Hope she won't notice that I used the whole bottle. Sort of.

Hallie: *[giggling]* You did?

Nora: And see the blue moon shells? I curved them around until they spelled your name. See?

Hallie: *[reaches in and pulls something out of the box]* What's this? Looks like Nancy Drew but . . .

Nora: It's the cover from one of my Nancy Drew books, *The Mystery of Moonstone Castle.*

Hallie: But that's your favorite. What did you do to it?

Nora: I just cut out her face. See? And then I cut up one of my school pictures. See? It's me.

Hallie: Oh, yeah.

Nora: And I just taped it under there. It didn't quite work exactly perfect.

Hallie: It's sort of funny.

Nora: I figured if it's a memory box of the summer, well you know . . .

Hallie: Know what?

Nora: That I have to be one, right. A memory. Of your summer.

Hallie: I guess so, but . . .

[NORA rushes on before HALLIE can interrupt.]

Nora: I mean, even if we're not friends anymore, you could remember when we played heroes, right? We never did get past Nancy Drew. But it was great, wasn't it?

Hallie: Yeah, it was.

Nora: Especially The Mystery of the Jade Dragon. That was the best. When you dressed me up in your mom's robe. *[NORA lifts up an imaginary robe, and HALLIE slowly slips her arms into its sleeves. The next sequence is played slowly, like a ritual, as they revisit the bows and the tea ceremony that had been part of this game.]*

Hallie: And we put those chopsticks in your hair.

Nora: And you painted all that eyeliner on me? And we walked around like this. *[bowing]*

Hallie: You looked so perfect!

Nora: Remember how we walked over to the lawn chairs, where all the adults were sitting and everyone was so surprised?

Hallie: And we had that official tea ceremony?

Nora: And all the little kids came to watch.

Hallie: And they tried to imitate us.

Nora: Until your little sister sent the tea set flying down the slide?

Hallie: You looked so great. And I took your picture on the stairs.

[The reminiscences stop abruptly when HALLIE remembers the broken camera.]

Before you smashed my camera, that is. Guess that's one more picture I won't have for my memory book.

Nora: But you can have the box.

Hallie: I don't want it. You're not even . . .

Nora: Not what?

Hallie: You're not my friend anymore.

Nora: *[trying feebly to make a joke]* But I can't take it back. It has your name on it. Who else am I going to give it to?

[MITCHELL enters and overhears this last bit. HALLIE and NORA don't notice him.]

Hallie: My dad yelled at me for half an hour for leaving it on the beach. Did you know that?

[HALLIE slowly and deliberately rips a shell off the cover of the echo box and smashes it with her foot.]

He won't get me another one until I save up all my allowance.

[She slowly rips off another shell and smashes it.]

Which will take me more than a year.

[She slowly rips off another shell and smashes it.]

And it's all your fault.

[HALLIE continues to ruin the box over the next few lines as NORA watches helplessly.]

Nora: It's not!

Hallie: You broke it.

Nora: I never did.

Hallie: If you didn't do it, then why did you make me this stupid box? If you weren't trying to pay me back for the camera?

Nora: I just wanted you to remember me.

Hallie: Remember you? I want to forget you.

Nora: But Hallie . . .

Hallie: I just don't want your stupid echo box. It'll just remind me that you're a liar.

[HALLIE starts to run out when MITCHELL stops her.]

SCENE TWELVE: HEROES

[MITCHELL grabs HALLIE by the arm.]

Mitchell: Hallie, wait up.

Hallie: What for?

Mitchell: Just take it.

[HALLIE tries to get away from him. They struggle over the next few lines, which come very fast.]

Hallie: Why should I? Let me go.

Mitchell: Because . . . because you just should.

Hallie: What are you talking about?

Nora: Let her go.

Hallie: Mitchell!

Nora: It doesn't matter.

Mitchell: Yes, it does. . . .

Nora: Just forget it, okay?

Mitchell: But she made it just for you.

Hallie: If you like the box so much, you take it. I don't even care.

[*HALLIE grabs the box from where she has thrown it and shoves it at MITCHELL.*]

This isn't your business anyway.

Mitchell: Yes, it is.

Hallie: Oh, yeah?

Mitchell: This is about the camera, right?

Hallie: I hate her. That's what it's about.

Mitchell: Because she broke it?

Hallie: [*nodding*] She wrecked my whole summer.

[*MITCHELL hands the box back to HALLIE.*]

Mitchell: Well, she didn't do it.

Hallie: You said you saw her.

Mitchell: I didn't.

Hallie: But you told me . . .

Mitchell: I lied.

Hallie: But then who? . . .

Mitchell: I did. . . . I did it, okay?

Hallie: What?

Mitchell: It was an accident. It was sitting on the ledge and I was fooling around. . . .

Hallie: Why did you . . .

Mitchell: I didn't see it . Look, I'm sorry. I really am, okay?

Hallie: But why'd you lie like that?

Mitchell: You thought it was her. So I just went along.

Hallie: I don't get it. Why?

Mitchell: Because once she got here, everything changed.

Hallie: No, it didn't.

Nora: *[quietly]* Hallie, I . . .

Mitchell: I'm sorry. . . .

Hallie: But everything's changed now.

> *[Pause. They look around. HALLIE, especially, is unsure what to do next. She has always looked up to MITCHELL, and this is very hard for her. She doesn't know how to make up with NORA either. She's stuck. NORA is struggling, too. The last thing she wants to lose is the opportunity to have two new friends. She decides to make the first move.]*

Mitchell: I'll just go now, eh?

Nora: Wait. . . .

> *[HALLIE looks from one to the other, then begins to pick up the broken shells.]*

Mitchell: I'll replace it, I promise. The camera, I mean.

Nora: Just wait a minute.

Mitchell: What for?

Nora: Leave those broken ones, Hallie. We can find you some more. Can't we, Mitchell? . . . Come on. . . .

> *[NORA crosses to MITCHELL.]*

Mitchell: No, I better go. . . .

Nora: Come on.

Mitchell: But I . . . Okay.

> *[MITCHELL and NORA start looking for shells. The beach is quiet as all three try to sort out their feelings.]*

Nora: Here's a pretty one.

Mitchell: Look how blue it is.

Nora: I love these abalone ones, don't you? They look like pearls.

Mitchell: I bet we can find more of those. What about under the dock?

[HALLIE is curious and moves in closer to the dock.]

Nora: Look, Hallie, we can use these to fix the box. If you want. I've got lots of glue left.

[HALLIE crouches down to join them. Pause.]

Look at this one Mitchell found. It's perfect, see?

[MITCHELL hands HALLIE the abalone shell.]

Mitchell: We can get more if you like . . . when the tide goes out.

Nora: And see? We can take these little ones and—

[In the distance, they can hear the loons approaching.]

Hallie: Listen.

Mitchell: The loons are coming back.

[Slowly, HALLIE climbs onto the dock and tries to take up the heron stand but loses her balance at first. NORA follows her lead eagerly, and as HALLIE shows her how to do it, she remembers how she learned it.]

Hallie: Just put all your weight on one leg.

Nora: Like this?

Hallie: Yeah. And stand as still as you can.

Nora: Okay.

Hallie: It just takes a little practice. Mitchell's the expert. He taught me.

[She reaches out her hand to MITCHELL and pulls him onto the dock. MITCHELL joins HALLIE in teaching NORA the heron stand.]

Mitchell: Just put your arm out for balance. That's right.

Hallie: You can reach over to one of us if you need to.

[All three stand on the dock, watching the horizon in the heron stand. Quiet.]

Hallie: You know what this is?

Mitchell: What?

Hallie: It's a Kodak moment. Too bad we don't have . . .

All together: A camera!

Hallie: Finally!

[They drop the heron stand, laughing, until a loon calls. It is close by.

They climb to the highest point on the dock, do a loon call, and wait.]

Mitchell: Perfect.

Nora: I know. You should get your tape recorder.

Hallie: Wait, I've got something better.

[HALLIE goes back for the echo box. She lays it down in front of the three of them, where it lies with its lid open.]

Okay, ready.

[They do one more loon call together.

Music up.

Fin.]

Moving Day

LINDSAY BURNS, NIKKI LUNDMARK, MARK LAWES / QUEST THEATRE PRODUCTION.

CHARACTERS
Willa
Nine years old and born fearless. Stubborn and full of ideas, generous, but always thinking of what's coming next. Used to being in charge.
Sam
Also nine years old. Eager, curious, loves to play, but a little shy with other kids.
Benji
Seven years old. High-spirited, accustomed to lots of action. Loves jokes and hates being left out.

SCENE ONE: THE JOURNEY

[WILLA enters. She is carrying three bags filled with stuff. She is completely absorbed in the list of things that she has and is checking them off out loud. This is the day she has been waiting for. She has been planning it for weeks, and the excitement of finally being able to put her plan into action is very visible. She is pumped.]

Willa: Okay. Okay. Okay. This is it! I think I have everything. . . . *[puts down the bags and starts rummaging through them]* Let's see. . . . I've got the flashlight. And the cookies. *[pulling out tinfoil]* I have the star-making stuff. And the bubble jar. *[A look of panic crosses her face.]* What about the confetti? Where's the confetti? Oh, no. . . . How could I forget the confetti? *[searches madly through the bags]* I can't believe this. . . . I really can't believe that I forgot the confetti. . . . Oh, no. . . . *[Enter SAM, carrying only one small bag. She can enter from behind the audience so that she has some distance to cover.]*

Sam: *[calling out]* Willa? Willa . . . are you out here?

Willa: I'm right here. Of course I'm here. I told you I'd be here, didn't I? It's the day we've been waiting for, isn't it? What did you think? That I'd be late?

Sam: No, I just . . . well, I didn't see you right away, that's all. I—

Willa: *[interrupting]* It's okay. Look, Sam, did you bring the confetti? I can't find it. I thought I had it in this bag but—

Sam: I've got it. You asked me to bring it, remember? Because I said we had some left from that New Year's party that my mom and dad had. *[pulling it out of her bag]* And I've got the lipstick and stuff, too. And some crackers. And these. . . .

Willa: Binoculars! Wow, what a great idea! These are the perfect thing for a clubhouse. No spies are going to be able to sneak up on us. *[hums theme from* Adam 12] Dum-de-dum-dum. . . . Dum-de-dum-dum . . .

Willa and Sam: *Dah!*

Sam: So are we ready to go or what?

Willa: To our first day?

Sam: At our magic clubhouse?

Willa: *[seriously and with great mystery]* By our very special route. *[gathers bags together]* Lady Aurora, are you ready?

Sam: Yes, Lady Filomena, I am ready.

[The audience can see an area set aside at the end of the alley. It has been marked somehow with a sign that says Keep Out. Club Members Only. When the audience first meets WILLA and SAM, the girls are only a few feet away from the clubhouse. However, their journey there takes a long time. The route is very circuitous, and every turn and twist the girls take has significance for them. Their words become very meaningful to them as they are drawn into the magic of their adventure. Their dialogue and actions become very dramatic.]

Willa: We have to go this way. Over the mountain to the valley of light.

Sam: And through the canyon of sand and wishes.

Willa: Silently moving past castle and hill.

Sam: Silently through the caves of time. *[crouching and crawling underneath the ladder]*

Willa: Holding the vision of our very own place.

Sam: Holding the vision of sisters united.

Willa: Holding the vision of future enchantments.

Willa and Sam: We enter the magic realm of . . .

[SAM falls and breaks the mood.]

Willa: Sam . . . look what you did. Now you broke the spell. We're going to have to start over!

Sam: But I had my eyes closed. I couldn't see where I was going. It's hard with your eyes closed.

Willa: Okay, okay. Let's not close our eyes. Let's say we wear these. . . . *[pulling two pairs of sunglasses out of the bag and handing one pair to SAM]* And we'll use the flashlight as our guide. *[pulls flashlight from bag]*

Sam: But it's light out!

Willa: Not in the magic forest, it isn't. It's the midnight hour, remember?

Sam: Oh, yeah. I forgot.

Willa: Are you ready?

Sam: Do we have to do the whole thing again? I want to hurry up and get there! I want to do the story.

Willa: *[exasperated]* Well, of course we have to do the whole thing again. That's what makes it magic, you pea-brain!

Sam: I am not a pea-brain! And if you start calling me names, Willa Barnes, I am just going straight home, and you can forget about having me in your stupid club. I don't need to listen to—

Willa: I didn't mean it. . . . I'm sorry. You're not a pea-brain.

You're my best friend!

Sam: Well, that's not a very nice thing to say to your best friend. Sometimes I really wonder if I'm your best friend. Sometimes you just make me feel stupid.

Willa: Oh, Sam. I'm sorry!

Sam: You're always sorry. You say this mean stuff, and then you're always sorry.

Willa: But you know you're my best friend. Ever since we were four years old. When you moved in next door to us. Remember?

Sam: Yeah.

Willa: And remember when you had to be in the hospital, and I sent you pictures I drew every day about what happened at school?

Sam: Yeah.

Willa: And remember when you told me that secret after we made that little apartment under the stairs, and I kept it even when I got in trouble with Mrs. Wilkinson?

Sam: Yeah!

Willa: You'll always be my best friend. I didn't mean to hurt you. I'll never call you another name. I swear.

Sam: No more names? Promise? *[slaps hand on leg, spits in palm, then offers hand to WILLA]*

Willa: No more names. Promise. *[slaps hand on leg, spits into palm, then shakes hands with SAM]*

Willa and Sam: Yuck! *[wipe hands on each other]*

Willa: Okay, look. What we'll do is . . . Well, what we'll do is, we'll speed it up.

Sam: How can we do that?

Willa: Well, we'll just do the words faster, and we'll leave out some of the journey part. Okay?

Sam: But will it still be magic?

Willa: If we concentrate really, really hard, it will be. Okay?

Sam: Okay.

[They put on the sunglasses. They move slowly, but their words come much faster than before.]

Willa: Lady Aurora, are you ready?

Sam: Yes, Lady Filomena, I am ready.

Willa: Over the mountain to the valley of light.

Sam: Through the canyon of sand and wishes.

Willa: Silently moving past castle and hill.

Sam: Silently moving through caves of time.

Willa: Holding the vision of our very own place.

Sam: Holding the vision of sisters united.

Willa: Holding the vision of future enchantments.

Willa and Sam: We enter the magic realm of time. We enter the magic realm of time. We enter the magic realm of time.

[They burst out laughing. Pause. They open an imaginary curtain.]

SCENE TWO: NO BOYS ALLOWED

[Now that WILLA and SAM have arrived in the clubhouse, their mood is jubilant. They start to unpack their belongings. It is clear this is their first real visit to the place. Their behavior conveys a definite sense of occasion.]

Sam: This is such a great place you found. Nobody is going to bug us here.

Willa: I know. Now it's time for us to decorate so we can have the ceremony in a little while.

Sam: The ceremony? But what about the story?

Willa: First, the ceremony. Remember we talked about what would make this into a magic place? Where magic things can happen? Did you bring that lemon stuff?

Sam: You mean this? [pulls a can of air freshener out of her bag] It really does smell pretty musty in here. Shall we try it?

[When WILLA nods, SAM starts to spray, but WILLA stops her.]

Willa: Wait, we can't just spray everywhere. This is magic air, remember? We have to have a saying.

[She picks up a scarf and holds the can high in the air.]

O, great wand!

Sam: O, great wand! *[squirt]*

Willa: *[moving around the clubhouse]* Keeper of all wisdom.

Sam: Keeper of all wisdom. *[squirt]*

Willa: Holder of all knowledge.

Sam: Holder of all knowledge. *[squirt]*

Willa: We initiate this magic place.

Sam: We initiate this magic place. *[squirt]*

[BENJI has entered and gets this last squirt in the face.]

Benji: Hey!

[WILLA and SAM chase BENJI around the clubhouse, eventually cornering him upstage.]

Willa: What are you doing here?

Benji: None of your business!

Willa: How did you find us?

Benji: I was looking for you guys for ages. Hey, what are you doing with that bathroom spray? Does Mom know you have it out here?

Sam: It's not bathroom spray, and it's from my house.

Willa: It's none of your business where it's from, you little geek. This is our clubhouse and you're not allowed.

Benji: Why not? Can't I just stay and—

Willa: *No!* You can't stay. We've been waiting all week for it to be Saturday so we could fix this place up to be our magic clubhouse. . . .

Benji: But I could—

Willa: We are planning a christening, Benji. And you have to go. . . . Right now.

Benji: But I won't get in the way. I promise. . . .

Sam: Sorry. No boys allowed.

Willa: *Out!*

Benji: But Willa . . . I was looking for you to tell you something. There's something going on at home. I know there is. Mom's been on the phone all day. . . .

Sam: Big deal! My mom's always on the phone.

Willa: Yeah, Benji. If you're so worried, ask Mom. Just get out of here!

Benji: But . . .

Sam: It's very dangerous here, you know.

Willa: Yeah. We've noticed lots of snakes.

Sam: It's not a place for little kids. *[squirts Benji with spray]*

Benji: I'm not afraid of snakes!

Willa: I don't care, Benji! Just get lost. *I mean it!*

[Willa pushes Benji out of the clubhouse. Benji tries to think of something to say, but can't and exits.]

Sam: I'm sure glad I don't have a little brother.

[Willa and Sam continue to unpack and fix things up.]

Scene Three: Argument

Willa: It's time we made some rules. Can't have everyone just barging in here.

Sam: So how do we figure out the rules?

Willa: It's our club! We just have to decide what's important to us.

Sam: Okay.

Willa: Like we don't want my geeky little brother in here. Or any of his little brat friends. And if anyone does sneak in . . . we'll squeeze their fingers into spaghetti!

Sam: No food unless it's shared?

Willa: That's a good one. Write that down. And in case someone did try to sneak up on us, we should have some kind of code word or something.

Sam: Code word?

Willa: Yeah. Remember when we were little and we had the blub-blub language?

Sam: Yeah. *[blows out her cheeks like a fish]* Blub-blub? *[meaning: Like this?]*

Willa: Blub. *[meaning: Yes]* Blub-blub-blub-blub-blub-blub-blub-blub-blub-blub-blub-blub. *[meaning: No one used to know what we were talking about.]*

Sam: Right. No one used to know what we were talking about!

Willa: So if we had just *one* word that we could say when we were with other people, they wouldn't know what we were talking about. Blub-blub-blub-blub-blub-blub?

Sam: I don't know what you're talking about.

Willa: Okay, so we're at your house and we're having supper with your whole family and I just happen to remember that we have to go to the clubhouse later, or else.

Sam: Or else what?

Willa: I don't know what else. Don't be so lame, Sam. Just listen. I'm trying to explain to you what a code word is. Blub? *[meaning: Okay?]*

Sam: Blub. *[meaning: Okay.]*

Willa: So you're asking me if I want the mashed potatoes or something and I say, "No, thanks, I'd rather have *strawberries.*"

Sam: But you love mashed potatoes.

Willa: Yeah, but what if *strawberries* was our password, you know, our code word?

Sam: Strawberries?

Willa: Yes! If I said, "No, thanks. I'd rather have *strawberries,*" you'd know I was talking about the clubhouse.

Sam: I would?

Willa: Yes, of course.

Sam: I might not though. Because if you said that at our

dinner table, everyone would just look at you funny. My dad's allergic to them so we never have them.

Willa: Allergic to what?

Sam: To strawberries!

Willa: You are not even listening. I don't care what the word is, as long as we have one. The point is not whether your dad is allergic to strawberries. The point is to have a *code word!*

Sam: You're yelling at me, Willa Barnes. You promised not to yell.

Willa: I'm sorry. I just want to organize a code word.

Sam: I want there to be a No Yelling rule in here.

Willa: Okay. *[writing it down]* Now, what about a code word?

Sam: Well, let's see. We both like 'em, so how about *mashed potatoes?*

Willa: Well . . . it's not very sophisticated. Or magical.

Sam: *[mimicking WILLA]* Well . . . I'm not very sophisticated. Or magical. And if you want me to like it, then that's what I'd like.

Willa: Mashed potatoes? *[starts to giggle]* Can you just see it? We'll be on the bus or something, or at school . . . and I'll turn to you and say *mashed potatoes* and no one will know what we're talking about.

Sam: Or else they'll think we're really hungry and all we can talk about is mashed potatoes!

Willa: And we could bring some potato mashers out here.

Sam: They could be our symbol!

Willa: We could be the Mashed Potato Club!

Sam: We could just be a couple of Mashed Potatoes! *[makes herself into the shape of a potato]* Potato.

Willa: *[follows SAM'S lead]* Potato. *[laughs]* Then we could get into a pot!

Sam: Okay. *[WILLA and SAM pretend to climb into a pot.]*

Then we add the water. *[They bob around, as if floating in water.]*

Willa: Oh, we're boiling now. We're boiling, boiling, BOILED! Arrgh! Here comes the *potato masher! [WILLA and SAM are mashed to the floor.]* I don't know about you, but I'm feeling pretty mashed right about now.

Sam: Me, too. It's a great name!

Willa: Let's make a sign.

Sam: I'll do it. You keep doing the rules. *[finds a large piece of cardboard and starts to draw sign]*

Willa: Okay, well, we have to figure out membership stuff.

Sam: Membership stuff?

Willa: Like who gets to be in the club. You know—what kind of people we want to have in our club.

Sam: But I thought—

Willa: *[interrupting]* Well, we already made one rule: No Boys. We want only girls, right?

Sam: Yeah, but when we first—

Willa: *[interrupting]* I think that should go right on the sign: No Boys. And I think that it should only be for girls who live in our neighborhood. You know, in case we have to have a meeting in a hurry, right?

Sam: Just wait a minute. I thought . . . Well, I thought we were just going to have a small club.

Willa: It can be small. We could have a limit. How many girls do you think we should have?

Sam: Well, I was thinking—

Willa: What about five? I think five would be a really good number, you know, because five would be about all we could fit in here, especially when we get mashed. *[giggling]* And if we want to have processions and stuff, it would get really crowded if—

Sam: *[interrupting]* But I thought it was just going to be us!

Willa: What?

Sam: I thought is was just going to be us two.

Willa: You mean just you and me?

Sam: Yeah. I thought we were going to be a club. Just us. You know, best friends.

Willa: Well, we can still be best friends and have other people in the club. It doesn't mean we wouldn't be best friends anymore if we asked Becca and Leanne or Emily to be in the club. . . .

Sam: Becca Underwood? You mean to tell me you would ask that . . . that . . . that . . . slime, Becca Underwood, to be in this club?

Willa: Well, I was only—

Sam: Don't you remember what she called me when we went swimming?

[SAM is upset but not yelling as she recalls this painful experience. She is just as upset that WILLA doesn't remember it.]

Willa: No, what . . .

Sam: You don't remember when I got that new silver bathing suit last summer, and I was wearing it at Riley Park?

Willa: I guess so. I . . .

Sam: Don't you remember what she said I looked like?

Willa: Like what?

Sam: *[pause]* Like a baby beluga whale, that's what!

Willa: But she was just kidding!

Sam: No, she wasn't! Her and her geek sister Angela were yelling after me, "Baby beluga in the deep blue sea—"

Willa: "—Swims so wild and swims so free!"

[SAM chases WILLA until she stops singing.]

Okay, okay, I remember. But that was way last summer. Look, we don't have to invite Becca. But we have to have some other members. It can't just be us. . . .

Sam: Why not? Why can't it just be us?

Willa: Because it's not a real club if we don't have members! I said we don't have to have Becca, if you're going to be a wimp about something that happened last summer.

Sam: A wimp? That's what you think I am? *[pause]* Well, you can just forget it, Willa Barnes. You can just find somebody else for your stupid club. And you can make yourself a new rule: No Wimps! *[packs up some of her stuff]*

Willa: Sam, wait up. . . . I didn't mean . . .

Sam: And while you're at it, you can just find yourself a new best friend, too! *[Sam throws her pack at Willa and runs out.]*

Willa: *[calling after Sam]* But I didn't mean it like that! *[waits for an answer]* I just got mad! *[waits]* I'm sorry! *[still no answer]* Well,l just go then. See if I care. This whole club was my idea anyway. I'm the *founder!* Why should I have to argue with anybody over these stupid rules? *[picks up list of rules]* No food unless it's shared. *[grabs a piece of licorice and starts to eat it]* Won't have to worry about that one anymore. Can have it all to myself! *[reads next rule]* No boys allowed. Easy! There won't be *anyone else* allowed! Except me! Introducing the Willa club! You can only join up if . . . if . . . if your name is Willa Barnes! *[throws rules down disparagingly]* The Mashed Potato Club . . . Hey! Wait a minute! I can pick my own code word now. And it can be as sophisticated and magical as I want it to be! It could even be *strawberries* after all! Whenever I say *strawberries*, no one will know what I mean . . . except me! It'll be my very own secret code word. *[tries whispering* strawberries *to herself, eating strawberries alone, passing herself secret strawberries]* "Oh, thank you very much. What's this? Oh, strawberries. . . . Don't eat them.

Strawberries, strawberries, the clubhouse, the clubhouse! *[nudge, nudge, wink, wink]* . . . I get it!" *[pause]*
That doesn't work! It's not a secret when I'm the only
one who knows it.

[WILLA pauses, moves somewhere else.]

Not very fun being the only member in my club. Even if
it's easier to get my own way. *[looks around, feeling
sorry for herself]* Sam? Sam? *[calling offstage]* Hey,
Sam? Wait up! Look, Sam. I'm sorry. Come back, okay?
[runs off]

SCENE FOUR: WE'RE MOVING

*[Music bridge to later that day. Benji enters, calling for
his sister.]*

Benji: Willa? Willa, I have to talk to you! I've got big news!
Willa? Are you out here?

*[He gives up, decides she isn't there. He looks around to
make sure no one is there and then makes his way into
the clubhouse. He starts poking around into stuff the
girls have left.*

*Meanwhile, SAM has entered. She hides, so BENJI doesn't
see her. BENJI picks up the air freshener and the binoculars. He mimics WILLA and SAM's ceremony by spray-
ing above his head.]*

Benji: *[squirt]* Oh, great wand! . . .

*[BENJI proceeds to play guns with the air freshener and
the binoculars. At one point, he throws his hat into the
air, firing at it. The hat should land down in front,
where SAM can pick it up easily. He continues to charge
around the clubhouse until he sees the rule book.]*

Benji: Rules. . . . Girls only. No boys allowed. . . . Who wants
to be in their sucky club anyway? *[squirts the rule book
with the spray]* No yelling. . . . *[looks around to make*

sure the coast is clear] Arrrgh! No food unless it's shared. . . . Well, that's a good one.

Sam: Any brothers caught in the club will be immediately beheaded. And their fingers will be made into spaghetti!

[SAM grabs BENJI's hat before he can get to it.]

Benji: I knew it was you.

Sam: So?

Benji: So what?

Sam: So what do you think you're doing in here?

Benji: I was just—

Sam: Can't you even read yet?

Benji: Yes, I can read. I was just—

Sam: Then you must know we don't allow boys.

Benji: But I—

Sam: Especially if it's somebody's little brother!

Benji: But this is important! This is top secret! I've got *big news!*

Sam: Like what?

Benji: I can't tell you. I have to find Willa. I've gotta hurry and find her.

[He starts to run off.]

Sam: Benji . . .

[She holds up BENJI's hat and taunts him with it.]

Benji: Hey! That's my hat.

[BENJI comes running back to get it.]

Sam: Come on! What is it?

[Sam crosses upstage and climbs the ladder, tempting BENJI to try to get his hat back. BENJI jumps into the clubhouse and tries twice to reach the hat.]

Benji: She's got to come home right away. Everything is haywire at home. . . .

Sam: Yeah?

Benji: My dad is all excited and my mom is crying. . . .

Sam: Why? What happened? *[no answer]* You've got to tell
    me. You're not getting out of here until you tell me, you
    little goober!

Benji: I can't tell you. Willa doesn't even know yet.

Sam: You have to tell me. *[starts to threaten him]* I'm Willa's
    best friend. Whatever it is, she's going to tell me right
    away. We don't keep any secrets. So tell me right now.

Benji: But I'm not supposed to. . . .

Sam: Tell me!

Benji: Well . . . we're moving!

Sam: Oh. Well, to a new house or what?

Benji: Nope. To Vancouver.

Sam: Vancouver?

Benji: Yeah. We get to go because my dad got transferred.

Sam: You mean you're leaving for good?

Benji: Yeah. *Forever.*

Sam: Forever? You mean you're not coming back?

Benji: Right.

Sam: Are you making this up? Because if you are . . .

Benji: I'm not. We're leaving in two weeks.

Sam: Two weeks?

Benji: Yeah. So you better tell Willa to come home. Mom
    and Dad need to tell her. I'm going to go start packing.
    Mom says we're gonna have a garage sale, and if I sell
    some toys and stuff, I can keep the money! See ya.
    [He runs out through the audience.]

Sam: To Vancouver?
    *[SAM sits alone in the clubhouse, toying with the signs.
    She starts to crumple some of them up. Music up.]*

SCENE FIVE: IT'S NOT ALWAYS TOGETHER
*[WILLA enters as SAM is starting to pick up some of her
stuff.]*

Willa: I knew you'd come back. You're just a warm little potato waiting to be mashed up, right?

Sam: Willa . . .

Willa: Look, I'm sorry about before. I got a little too excited about the rules. We can be the only members if you want. Just you and me, okay?

Sam: Willa . . .

Willa: Yeah, just us. Besides, I only got two potato mashers. Look! I got them from your mom when I went over to your house looking for you.

Sam: Did my mom tell you something? Some news or anything?

Willa: No. Why?

Sam: Never mind. Just wondering.

Willa: *[She proudly pulls out a new sign she has made for the clubhouse that reads Best Friends Only and props it up.]* See what I brought?

Sam: Willa . . .

Willa: So we can forget about it? The fight, I mean?

Sam: I guess so. Do you promise to be my best friend—no matter what?

Willa: No matter what. Hey . . . what's with you?

Sam: Nothing. . . . I just—

Willa: Okay, then let's get ready for the ceremony. You know, the christening ceremony. We have to christen the clubhouse. We have to make it ours. Best friends only. Right?

Sam: I guess.

Willa: *[excited and quite oblivious to SAM's mood]* Okay, then. Let's get started. We have to get all dressed up. I have some stuff in here for us to wear. Oh. Close your eyes. . . .

Sam: Willa . . .

Willa: Close your eyes. Go on. . . . *[puts a bracelet on SAM's wrist]* There! It's a present. For you.

Sam: For me? Really?

Willa: I made it myself.

Sam: Oh, this is really harsh. I love it. All this twirly stuff. Did you really make it just for me?

Willa: Yeah. It was supposed to be for your birthday, but I wanted you to have it to celebrate today. For the christening.

[SAM admires her bracelet and watches as WILLA unloads one of the bags she brought in during the first scene.]

Willa: And look what I've got!

[WILLA pulls a large plastic bag full of makeup out of the bag.]

Sam: Wow! Where did you get all that makeup?

Willa: My mom has a drawer full of this junk in the bathroom that she never even uses. She said I could fool around with it. As long as I don't wear it to school. This purple lipstick will look great on you. *[hands the lipstick to SAM along with a small hand mirror]* And I even have some silver eye shadow. You're gonna look so great. *[starts to put eye shadow on SAM]* Oh! We'd better get started on a chant for the christening. It has to be something real special. Let's see. Say it after me so I can hear how it sounds, okay?

Sam: Okay.

Willa: Over the mists and sands of time.

Sam: Over the mists and sands of time.

Willa: Two best friends sworn together.

Sam: Two best friends . . .

Willa: Holding the vision of their very own place . . . Always together, never apart.

Sam: It is not.

Willa: No, listen. . . . Always together, never apart!

Sam: It is not!

Willa: Not what? What's the matter?

Sam: It's *not* always together! It's not two best friends sworn together either! Always together. It's not!

Willa: It is so. I said I was sorry. I promised it would just be us. Not Becca or Leanne or anybody else. Just best friends . . .

Sam: But you won't be anymore.

Willa: What are you talking about?

Sam: I can't tell you. You're supposed to go home.

Willa: Why? What's the matter?

Sam: It's a secret. Your mom has to tell you.

Willa: But we have no secrets, remember? You have to tell me!

Sam: I can't.

Willa: Best friends don't have secrets. Tell me!

Sam: But you can't be my best friend anymore.

Willa: Yes I can.

Sam: No you can't!

Willa: Why not?

Sam: Because you'll be gone!

Willa: Gone? Where?

Sam: To Vancouver, that's where! You're moving there!

Willa: What? I don't know what you're talking about.

Sam: Benji was here. He said you're moving. In two weeks.

[Willa is hit hard. For once, she is uncertain what to do next.]

Willa: But my mom never said . . .

Sam: They just found out. You're supposed to go home.

Willa: I'd better . . . I'd better just . . . *[runs out]*

[After Willa leaves, Sam is still upset and alone onstage. She takes off the bracelet and calls after Willa.]

Sam: Just go! Don't even bother coming back! You can just

forget all about this stupid club. Just like you're going to forget all about me!

[SAM runs out. Music up.]

SCENE SIX: BENJI'S MONOLOGUE

[BENJI enters.]

Benji: My dad says we'll get a sailboat. And we'll just jump in it on Saturdays and take off. Maybe we'll go to Hawaii, just me and my dad. And I'm going to learn to ski. My mom's a really good skier, you know. And you know how we have to drive all the way to Banff to get to the mountains? Well, in Vancouver, we're going live right *in* the mountains. In fact, our new house is probably going to be at the very top of a mountain. We'll probably have to ski down to school. We'll probably have to ski everywhere!

[BENJI mimics skiing as he exits.]

SCENE SEVEN: I AM STAYING HERE

[SAM enters and starts to pack away her stuff.]

Sam: Rules. Stupid list of rules. She was always the one making up rules. She is so bossy. This isn't even magic anyway. Willa Barnes and all her stupid ideas. Always making up magic stuff and chants. She is so weird. Half of this stuff is mine. She probably thinks she can just take all of it with her. To Vancouver! She always gets her own way. . . . Best friends. Oh, sure.

[WILLA enters carrying a box of stuff.]

Willa: Hi.

Sam: Hi.

[They look at each other glumly.]

Willa: I'm sorry. . . .

Sam: Sorry I yelled at you like that.

Willa: That's okay.

Sam: It's not really your fault. . . . About moving I mean.

Willa: It's my dad's fault. He cares more about his stupid job than he cares about me, that's for sure. And my mom is even worse. She expects me to just throw out half of my stuff. *[indicating box]*

Sam: You mean all of this beautiful stuff?

Willa: Well, we went through everything. And there's, like, eight million boxes of stuff she's just throwing away.

Sam: Like this one?

Willa: No. This is a Maybe Box. It's for the stuff we haven't decided on yet. Maybe we'll keep it. Maybe we won't.

Sam: So do you get to decide or what?

Willa: Yeah. *[digging around in the box]* Hey, remember this? *[pulls out a couple of sticker books]* We were so into stickers. The *Snow White* ones.

Sam: The *Jem* ones.

Willa: And the *Smurfs!*

Sam: We used to trade them all the time. And sometimes we'd fight.

Willa: Of course we were just little then. That was way last summer.

Sam: Look at this! Remember, you got this for Christmas from your Auntie Agnes? *[pulling out an old stuffed animal]* And you hated it!

Willa: Yeah, but I got to like it after a while. I called it Smoochie.

Willa and Sam: Smoochie, smoochie!

Sam: Hey, I remember this hat. *[pulls a battered, old-fashioned ladies hat from the box]* You used to have that great dress-up box, remember?

Willa: You can have it, if you want.

Sam: The hat? Really, you mean it?

Willa: Yeah. I can't believe my mom wants me to just pitch this stuff out. I don't even want to go home. I can't stand watching her destroy our house. At least she can't wreck the clubhouse.

Sam: Well, why don't we use the stuff? Here, I mean. We can use it to decorate the clubhouse.

[They both start to place the various items around the space.]

This is going to look great.

Willa: Yeah, it's just going to be perfect. It's got everything we need. *[pulling out a large sheet of fabric]* Hey, look at this. I can make a bed. . . . I don't even have to go home. I should just sleep here. I could hide out here. They can just leave for Vancouver without me!

Sam: That's a great idea! I'll bring you meals every day. Licorice. Gum. And chocolate chip cookies. Everything you need!

Willa: And water. I'll need some water.

Sam: Okay. What else?

Willa: A housecoat. It's getting cold out here.

Sam: Right. And I'll bring you some hot chocolate. With marshmallows! I'll use my sister's *Ghostbusters* thermos. And I'll bring some Slurpees and comics. And videos! I'll get some videos. With popcorn and—

Willa: Sounds great. I can just stay here forever. Oh. I'll have to write my mom and tell her I'm running away.

Sam: Here. Use the rule book.

Willa: Great!

Sam: Okay. I'll go and get everything right now. *[starts to leave]* Willa?

Willa: What?

Sam: I'm really glad you're staying.

[SAM exits.]

Willa: Dear Mom, I am writing to tell you good-bye. I am not coming to Vancouver. No way. *[pause]* I am staying here with my best friend in the world, Sam. Don't worry about me. I have a wonderful new house to live in, and I'm going to have lots to eat. Love, Willa. P. S. Say good-bye to dad for me. Hope he likes his new job.

[WILLA finishes the letter, folds it up, and puts it to one side. During the next speech she moves around, picking up the items she mentions and preparing her bed.]

Willa: Got everything I need right here. Got my Smoochie and my flashlight, so I won't be afraid at night. And I'll be able to see the stars at night. And Sam will be here every day. We could have sleep overs out here. Uh-oh. I don't have my toothbrush. Oh, well. Sam can bring it to me. I can use all this stuff for my bed, and I can make my bed right over here.

[WILLA sets up her bed and lies down to sleep.]

SCENE EIGHT: OGOPOGO STORY

[BENJI enters carrying a hockey stick, a backpack, and a sleeping bag. He sees his sister in the clubhouse. He is visibly upset about something.]

Benji: Willa? . . . Willa? . . . Are you awake?

Willa: No, I'm not.

Benji: Can I come in? Just for a minute?

Willa: I guess so. . . . Just this once, though. *[He starts to come in.]* Hey, wait a minute. You can't just crawl in here any old way. Don't you remember? This is a club-house.

Benji: Oh, yeah. I forgot. *[goes around to the entrance]*

Willa: We've got rules, you know. *[starts to clear away her "bed"]* Hey! *[She indicates the correct way to enter. BENJI complies.]* What are you doing with all that junk?

Benji: *[after a pause]* I'm not going to Vancouver. I'm running away.

Willa: What? You have to go! That's all you've been talking about. "I can't wait till moving day! I can't wait till we go to Vancouver!"

Benji: Yeah. . . . Well . . .

Willa: Did something happen? *[BENJI doesn't answer.]* Come on. What is it?

Benji: Well . . . I was telling Stuart about how we're moving to Vancouver, and his brothers came and started bugging me.

Willa: Those guys are such jerks. What did they say?

Benji: They said that in B.C. there's an *Ogopogo* monster. Is that true?

Willa: Yeah, I've heard of it. I think I saw it on TV once. Why?

Benji: Well, Stuart's brothers said . . .

Willa: Said what? Come on. Tell me. . . .

Benji: They said that it . . .

Willa: What?

Benji: That it likes to eat little kids.

Willa: Ah, Benj. I don't think so. They're such jerks! . . . You know what this reminds me of? Remember when we were little? Whenever we used to be scared of something, Mom would say it's time to fight the Worry Monster! *[grabs the sleeping bag]* She'd say, "Take that, Worry Monster!" And it would go away! *[pause]* We've got a lot of worries now, don't we, Benj? Moving to Vancouver . . .

Benji: Going to a new school . . .

Willa: Saying good-bye to our best friends . . .

Benji: Hiding from the Ogopogo . . .

[Pause. WILLA looks around the clubhouse, then at BENJI.]

Willa: Or being ready for the Ogopogo!

Benji: Ready for what?

Willa: Ready to look him in the eye! You don't think I'm going to let any old monster eat you up, Benji. You're my brother! *[grabs the hockey stick and slashes at the "monster"]* Take that, you stupid monster. Take that! *[to BENJI]* You tell Stuart's jerk brothers that your sister, Willa, is going to take care of any old monster.

[They both bash around with sticks.]

That's what sisters are for!

[SAM enters with a box of stuff.]

Sam: Hey, what's going on here? No boys allowed, remember?

Benji: But I was just . . .

Willa: It's okay, Sam. I was just showing Benji some moves. *[to BENJI]* Why don't you go get that battle junk you have? You know, in the garage?

Benji: Okay. *[He exits.]* I'll be right back.

Sam: He's coming back? But what about the rules? No boys, remember? Especially brothers?

Willa: Sam, it's okay. It's okay.

Sam: Oh. Well, wait till you see all the stuff I brought you. *[starts to pull out cereal and other stuff from her box]* I've got Honeycomb Cereal and Kraft Dinner for lunch and gum—

Willa: *[grandly]* I am very thankful for your kindness, Lady Aurora.

Sam: You are very welcome, Lady Filomena.

Willa: But it can wait until just a little bit later, my dear. Now it is time for . . .

Sam: For what?

Willa: For the story.

Sam: Oh, great! Your turn or mine?

Willa: *[dreamily]* Mine. *[Both girls get settled.]* There once was a kingdom where there lived two fairy princesses.

Sam: I love princess ones.

Willa: One was named Filomena and the other was . . .

Sam: Aurora.

Willa: Right. Filomena and Aurora both had golden hair down to their knees. They were very strong and rode horses whenever they wanted. They slept on feather beds, and every morning that's where they ate their breakfast of chocolate and . . .

Sam: Grapes.

Willa: Yes. *[mimes feeding a grape to Sam]* Early one morning, as they were eating their breakfast, there was an urgent message . . .

Sam: *[standing up]* From the Queen.

Willa: *[standing as well]* Right. And because they were strong and loyal princesses . . .

Sam: They were always ready to serve their queen . . .

Willa: Whenever there was trouble.

Sam: So they opened up the urgent message.

Willa: Which said, "The kingdom faces an emergency. The queen needs someone to go off and fight the secret monster."

Sam: The Secret Monster?

Willa: And Filomena was chosen to go because she was brave and she could ride her horse faster than anyone.

Sam: But what about Aurora? They always go riding off together.

Willa: Not this time. Only one could go.

Sam: But they were partners!

Willa: They had to remember that they were brave and strong. One had to be brave enough to go but—

Sam: But I want to go, too!

Willa: And one had to be brave enough to stay. Before she rode off, Filomena made a pact with Aurora.

Sam: Never to forget each other?

Willa: Never to forget each other.

Sam: Always to remember?

Willa: Always to remember.

Sam: Holding the vision of their very own place?

Willa: Holding the vision of their very own place.
    [Pause.]

Sam: But I don't want to stay here alone. I don't want you to go!

Willa: I don't want to go either. I'm scared.

Sam: I want you to stay!

Willa: I know, but I can't.

Sam: But why not? You can stay here, in the clubhouse. . . .

Willa: I can't. Benji needs me. Can't be scared. I have to be . . . like Filomena!

Sam: Brave, you mean. Like Aurora has to be?

Willa: Yeah, just like them. *[pause]* It's not far to Vancouver, you know. My mom says it's only a couple of hours on the plane.

Sam: Or a day on the train. We rode the train once.

Willa: You could come out at Christmas. We could go skiing.

Sam: And you could come for summer holidays. For the Stampede.

Willa: We could write lots of letters. You can tell me about everybody at school.

Sam: We could use the code!

Willa: Yeah! Blub-blub letters!

SCENE NINE: THE BATTLE

[BENJI enters, carrying a garbage can shield, pole, and sword. He is wearing an ice-cream pail as a helmet.]

Benji: *Charge!*

Willa: Benji!

Benji: Got everything we need.

Willa: For the great battle?

Sam: What great battle?

Willa: With the Ogopogo. Right, Benj?

Sam: Ogopogo?

Benji: We're gonna slay the dragon. Willa's going to help me. You can, too, if you want.

Willa: *[to SAM]* It's the Moving Day Monster! *[to BENJI]* You know, I was thinking. This Ogopogo is a sea monster, right?

Benji: Right. He lives at the bottom of the sea, and the only time he comes to the surface is when he's really mad.

Willa: Well, we don't want to wait for that to happen. We want to take him by surprise.

Sam: How will we do that?

Willa: We'll make a ship! And we'll sail out to meet him.

Sam: Good idea!

Benji: We can use this as a mast!

Willa: Benji, toss me that wheel.

Sam: We'll need a sail. . . .

[Through the next few lines, they gather up sticks, sheets, ropes, and move to make the clubhouse into a sailing ship. The mast of the ship does not go completely up until the final moments of the play, so it can serve as a signal of change.]

Benji: Timber!

Willa: This is going to be great! Yo-ho-ho and a bottle of rum! Hey, look at this!

[WILLA finds a cardboard roll, which she uses as a telescope. She also discovers a piece of material, which she turns into a pirate headband.]

Excellent!

Sam and Benji: Sail's ready!

Willa: Hoist the sails!

Sam and Benji: Hoist the sails!

Willa: We've got to meet him head on. Captain's orders! All hands on deck! Cast off!

Benji: Sail's up, Captain. We are the sailors of the Seven Seas.

Sam: We're off to meet the enemy.

Willa: Sailing into the future.

Sam: Over the mists and sands of time.

Benji: Captain, I think I'm gonna puke!

Willa: Oh, gross, Benji! . . . Wait a minute! Wait a minute! I think I see something. . . .

Sam: See what?

Willa: It's the monster!

Sam: What's he doing?

Willa: He's circling.

Benji: What's he look like?

Willa: He's huge!

Benji: Let me see! Let me see!

Sam: He's green!

Benji: Let me see! He's slimy!

Willa: He's gigantic!

Sam: What's he doing now?

Willa: He sees us! Crew members, prepare for battle!

Sam and Benji: Battle positions! Battle positions!

Benji: Is he coming? Is he going to chase us?

Sam: He sees us coming! Everybody stand by!

Willa: Get your weapons! All hands on deck!

Sam: Hey, guys! We could use this as a harpoon.

Willa: Great idea! Quick, Benji, get up on my shoulders.

Sam: Hurry, hurry, he's coming! He's coming. *[They try to harpoon the monster.]* He's coming up! He's coming up!

Get him! . . . Quick. Over this way. Here he is! Here he
is! Get him!

Benji: I got him! He's got us! Arrgh!

Sam: What happened?

Benji: I lost him.

Sam: Where is he?

Willa: Wait a minute, wait a minute. . . .

Benji: What's he doing?

Willa: I can't see him.

Sam: Where is he?

Willa: He's quiet. . . . He's waiting. . . .

All: *He's under the boat!*

*[The action now speeds up considerably. Props and
actors go flying as the "monster" rocks the boat from
side to side. Benji mimics being thrown overboard.]*

Willa: Red alert! Red alert!

Benji: Help! Man overboard! Help!

Sam: Quick, Benj. Grab this. . . . *[tries to reach BENJI with
the sword]*

Benji: He's got my leg!

Willa: You let go of my little brother! Take that, you monster! Watch out. There are three of us!

*[All grab some sort of weapon with which to beat off the
monster.]*

Benji: You can't get us! We're not scared of you!

Willa: Wait a minute! . . . Wait a minute! . . . He's doing something. . . . He's swimming. . . . He's swimming away!

Sam: Hooray! We did it!

Benji: We beat him. We beat the monster.

Sam: He could see we were ready for him.

Willa: He could see we were ready. We were united.

Sam: United and strong.

Benji: We scared him away! We really scared him!

All: Hooray!

Willa: Hoist the sails!

Sam and Benji: Hoist the sails!

Willa: Coast is clear. . . . Disaster over. . . . Smooth sailing ahead.

[Pause. They look around. Music starts up.]

Sam: It's great up here.

Willa: I can see for miles.

Benji: I can see the stars.

Sam: I can see forever.

Willa: I have seen the future. And it's big.

Sam: We can sail into it.

Willa: Holding the vision of sisters . . .

Benji: And brothers . . .

Willa: And brothers, united.

Sam: Holding the vision of future enchantments.

Willa: Unafraid of new tomorrows! *[dreamily]* We enter the magic realm of time.

Sam: *[determinedly]* We enter the magic realm of time.

Benji: *[like a battle cry]* We enter the magic realm of time!

[Music up.

Fin.]

Willa and Sam

CHARACTERS

Sam

Twelve years old. Eager to resume her friendship with WILLA. SAM *is curious about the world and what makes it work. She has a very active inner life and remains comfortable with playing and pretending. She is a very grounded person in many ways and loves to have fun and ask questions. She is an only child and has always been able to play on her own. Sam is the kind of kid you might label a loner.*

Willa

Also twelve years old, but at this point in her life, she is twelve going on fifteen. She is trying to be as grown up as she can. The problem is that she's unsure about what that means. She has lost some of her physical confidence and has gone from being the leader to being the follower. Suddenly, what she wears and who she's with have become very important to her. She's entered new territory, and she is not sure where she fits in anymore. Her solutions are to overcompensate and become defensive.

Benji

Nine years old. Although he is always eager to please, he loves jokes and eavesdropping on his sister. He's at that age when everything is an adventure. Benji adapted well to the move to Vancouver and is just as excited about moving back to Calgary as he was about moving to Vancouver. He is resilient and always has been.

Except for the opening sequences, the play is set in SAM'S *back yard in Calgary, where* WILLA *and her brother,* BENJI, *are moving after spending three years in Vancouver. All three characters are from* Moving Day, *which was about having to say good-bye to your best friend and conquering the fears that everyone has of the unknown.* Willa and Sam *looks at the fragile territory between childhood and the teen years.*

SCENE ONE: LETTER TO WILLA

[Playground space in Calgary. It's not a formal playground but there is a jungle gym and a picnic table. This is part of the shared outdoor space for several houses, including SAM's and the house where WILLA and BENJI used to live. It is beside a garage with lumber, old tires and other junk lying around.

SAM runs in holding an envelope in her hands. She settles in at her favorite spot at the picnic table and opens an envelope that obviously has already been opened many times. Reads aloud from the letter she has received from WILLA.]

Sam: "Sam, I think we'll probably get there on the first of July. Yes! It will be nice to see you again. Do you remember our clubhouse? Love, Willa."

Do I remember?

[SAM reads aloud from the letter she has already written in response and is about to mail. She is not writing as she speaks but reading it over one last time before she mails it.

WILLA enters and gets same letter out of the mailbox. She sits down on the porch swing at her house in Vancouver.]

"Dear Willa, there are new houses across the street in the field where our clubhouse used to be. But how could I forget? Those were the best times!

I can hardly believe you're moving back home. You'll be here in two more weeks! I can't wait ! I think I'm going to explode. It'll be just like one of those aliens on the *X-Files.*

[Sploosh, wham noises.

Music up as SAM *writes and reads out loud.]*

I told the *world* you were coming back. All your old friends. Of course I'm the only one who wrote all the time.

*[*SAM *exits.* WILLA *continues to read the letter.]*

Willa: "The Fergusons? You know, those people who rented your house while you were gone? They moved out yesterday, so your place is all ready for you."

*[*BENJI *enters, listening in. He is wearing hiking boots and a backpack.]*

"I just keep looking across the playground at your old house and imagining you back in it. I want to go up and say, 'Knock, knock. Anybody home?' Remember all the knock, knock jokes we used to do?"

Benji: I've got one. Knock, knock.

Willa: Sneaking up me again! Why don't you just—

Benji: Mom told me to find you.

Willa: What for?

Benji: You're supposed to go in and help label more boxes.

Willa: As if I haven't been her slave all day.

*[*WILLA *starts to enter the house, but* BENJI *blocks her way.]*

Benji: Knock, knock.

*[*WILLA *tries to get past him, but he blocks the way again.]*

Knock, knock. *[won't let her go in the house until she listens to his joke]*

Knock, knock.

Willa: All right. Who's there?

Benji: An annoying brown cow.

Willa: An annoying—

Benji: Moo.

Willa: An annoying brown—

Benji: Moo.

Willa: An annoying brown—

Benji: Moo . . . annoying. Get it?

Willa: Not bad, Benji. Now can I just get by?

Benji: Oh, sure. Have fun labeling boxes!

[WILLA exits.]

Make sure you're extra careful with mine. I already packed up all my Power Ranger stuff. Wait till Kevin and Jeff see all the new ones I got. And these new hiking boots. *[does some kind of hiking warm-up with his new boots]* My mom and dad said that since we're moving back to the mountains, they're going to take us hiking in the Kananaskis this summer. We're going to carry our tent and everything and camp above the treeline. I've been putting rocks in my backpack. You know, to get in shape.

[BENJI begins to exit. He is playing at climbing a mountain.]

We'll probably climb at least one mountain a day. Maybe two. By the end of the summer, we'll probably have climbed every single peak in the Rocky Mountains. Nothing is impossible. Now that I've got the boots!

[BENJI exits.]

SCENE TWO: SAM'S TAPED LETTER IN CALGARY / WILLA'S REPORT IN VANCOUVER

[Scene takes place in both cities. SAM is in Calgary in the play area beside the garage. WILLA is speaking in front of her class in Vancouver. We hear whale sounds as SAM enters carrying a big piece of gray fabric, a sewing basket, and a bag holding her tape recorder, markers, and so on.

Some quiet onstage time as she proudly gets the fabric ready to hang up. SAM puts her tape recorder on the picnic table, inserts a tape, and begins to speak as she hangs the fabric on the clothesline attached to the garage. The audience sees the outline of a whale.]

Sam: Hi, Willa. . . . This will be the last letter I tape to you because you won't be in Vancouver anymore. You'll be here . . . duh. . . .

[Whale sounds fade out while the sounds of a classroom come up in another part of the playing area. WILLA is working on a report for her Vancouver classmates.]

Willa: Mr. Sangster is letting me do this . . . report/speech as my final assignment because we're leaving the day after tomorrow and I couldn't get my essay finished. It's called . . . "Moving Again."

Sam: I'm doing Orcas for the science fair the last week of school. Everything's ready. I started to make a puppet to use as a decoration, but it won't be done in time. I'll get it done this summer.

I'm using these whale-sound tapes my dad sent from Blackfish Sound. I wish he'd invite me out there for a visit. Did I tell you I have a baby stepsister I haven't even met yet? Guess my dad is pretty busy with stuff. Maybe next summer.

Willa: My dad has to go back to his old job in Calgary. Either that or he loses it, right? Two and a half years ago, we move all the way here, change our entire lives and now—poof! We have to just go back again as if nothing happened. Not.

Sam: For Christmas my mom made me an adoptive parent of a whale. It's not like I'm the only parent or anything. Or even that I'll get to meet her. It's just a donation, right? But I got a certificate and a little pin. Her name is Star.

Willa: It was suppertime when my dad told us. I couldn't swallow. Just left the table. Not the dweeb though. That's my brother, Benji. He'll eat anywhere, anything, anytime. Like, on Friday night we had a going away party, a sleep over at my house. My mom made all this food. Like, angel food cake. Pizza with ham and pineapple. Nachos. I don't know what she was thinking! Like, we can eat stuff like that anymore. As if! We'd be blimps. Like Roseanne!

Sam: I want to live on the water. Maybe I'll have my own houseboat. When I'm a marine biologist like my dad, I can spend all my time studying whales, swimming with them. Saving them!

Willa: My mom just doesn't get it. She kept on asking me all week, "What games are you going to play?" Hello, mother. . . . We're twelve! And the video she rented? My friends wanted to see *Speed!* I told her that, but what does she get? *The Incredible Journey.* I wanted to crawl underground I was so embarrassed.

Sam: Katie called me and asked if I was having a party to welcome you home. I told her no. It would be fun but maybe later in the summer. You'll probably be tired when you got here. And you'll have all that unpacking to do and everything.

Willa: So the food honked. The video honked. We were so-o-o-o-o-o bored. Luckily, Courtenay brought over her new CD player. So we listened to the Cranberries, watched my little brother eat almost all the food. It was ultra disgusting.

Sam: I can't wait to show you all my whale stuff. And I'll play you the tapes from Blackfish Sound. The whales . . . they sound sad, you know? So lonely. As if they didn't have a friend in the world.

[Whales sounds come back up.]

Willa: You want to know what my perfect fantasy is for when that moving van pulls away tomorrow?

Sam: I'd better get this in the mail so you'll get it before you leave. See you soon. And I really mean that!

Willa: That my little nimrod brother gets mysteriously left behind. That's it. Thank-you.

[Classroom sounds come back up. WILLA and SAM exit.]

SCENE THREE: EN ROUTE TO CALGARY

Voice-over of flight attendants: Good morning ladies and gentlemen, and welcome to Canadian Airlines flight 682 service to Calgary and Toronto. Please make sure your carry-on luggage is stored safely in the overhead compartments. We are scheduled to land in Calgary at approximately 9:40 A.M. The captain has informed me that the weather in Calgary this morning . . .

[BENJI is seated beside WILLA, playing with the barf bag, fooling around with the belts. WILLA looks annoyed that she has to sit with him.]

Benji: Isn't this just the best? Look how it works.

Willa: My worst nightmare. Stuck beside you for ninety-five minutes.

Benji: When do we eat?

Willa: We just ate. You had a hamburger, french fries, pizza, onion rings . . .

Benji: And a peach milkshake . . . Willa?

Willa: What?

Benji: I think I'm gonna be sick.

Willa: You are not.

Benji: Yeah, I am. I think it was the peach milkshake.

Willa: You are not.

Benji: I am so. I just know it.

Willa: Quit being such a little jerk.

Benji: I'm gonna hurl any minute.

Willa: Stop it. You are not.

Benji: Yes, I am. You better get Mom.

Willa: Can you just talk a little louder? I don't think the pilot heard you.

Benji: You better move over. This isn't gonna be pretty.

Willa: Here. Take this.

Benji: What is it?

Willa: It's a barf bag.

Benji: You mean it's full of barf? Grosserama!

Willa: It's not full of barf.

Benji: Yet. What's in here then?

Willa: It's empty, you little stain. So you can barf in it.

Benji: You mean right here?

Willa: Yes! Just do it.

Benji: I can just let it rip?

Willa: Just do it.

Benji: Right here? Right now? Hundreds of miles above the earth?

Willa: Yes! Just do it and shut up!

[BENJI starts heaving into the bag. WILLA is mortified. She tries to shrink into her seat. BENJI puts it on for a minute, then starts to laugh.]

Benji: Gotcha.

Willa: You little . . .

Benji: Brother. I'm your little brother. Aren't you glad?

Willa: I'm going to get you. . . .

Benji: And when we get back to Calgary? And you have no friends?

Willa: Would you just shut—

Benji: You'll always have me.

Willa: I could—

Benji: And my barf bag. I'm going to keep it. As a souvenir.

[Music and airplane sound up. BENJI and WILLA chase each other out.]

SCENE FOUR: REUNION

[SAM is finishing hanging up a Welcome Home banner for WILLA. BENJI enters, sneaks up on her, and throws a paper airplane at her.]

Sam: Benji!

Benji: Hey, you forgot my name.

Sam: Benji!

Benji: It should read Welcome Home Willa and Ben. It's Ben. Or Welcome Home Ben and Willa.

Sam: You got taller.

Benji: Or just Welcome Home Ben. That's even better.

Sam: When did you get here?

Benji: This morning. We flew all the way here. Boy, are my arms tired!

Sam: I forgot about your jokes.

Benji: *[throws the paper airplane again]* Do you know what?

Sam: What?

Benji: I was even invited into the cockpit to see how the pilots fly the plane. I could do that. *[plays out the whole landing with the paper plane]*
Approaching the runway now. Air traffic Control. Can you read me? *[to SAM]* Well, come on!

Sam: Air Traffic Control to Pilot Barnes. Welcome to Calgary.

Benji: Permission to land, Air Traffic Control.

Sam: Your runway is clear. You can make your approach.

Benji: Thank-you, Air Traffic Control. We are coming full speed ahead. Here we go. . . . Touch down. Another smooth landing.

[BEN lands the plane, cheers for himself. SAM picks it up.

They land on the ground somehow. SAM picks up the airplane.]

Sam: How'd you learn to make it?

Benji: On the plane. They gave us this little booklet deal, and it had directions for making all different kinds of planes.

Sam: Cool.

[SAM keeps fingering the plane over the next sequence, turning it around and upside down, trying to see how it works.]

Benji: The booklet had all sorts of airplane stuff. Even jokes.

Sam: Uh-oh.

Benji: Like . . . Where does an airplane put its jacket?

Sam: I dunno.

Benji: On an airplane hanger! Pretty good, eh!

Sam: Well . . .

Benji: What has four wheels and flies?

Sam: I dunno.

Benji: A garbage truck!

Sam: Groaner.

Benji: Okay, here's the best one. Why did the mayonnaise miss its flight?

Sam: Why?

Benji: Can't you guess?

Sam: No.

Benji: Because it was dressing! Get it? Because the mayonnaise was dressing.

[SAM laughs and then sits quietly looking at the plane. BENJI picks it up and starts to show her how to fly it.]

Benji: I could show you how to make these if you like.

Sam: Would you? That'd be great.

Benji: Sure. All I need is some big flat paper. See? The big ones fly the best.

[They are flying the planes around when WILLA enters.]

Willa: *[offstage]* Benji? Are you out here? Oh, there you are. I'm supposed to come and get you. . . . Oh, hi.

Sam: Willa! Hi!

Willa: I didn't know you were . . .

Sam: Welcome home! Do you like it?

Willa: Like what?

Benji: The banner, doofus. She made it for you.

Willa: Well, yeah. It's so . . . sweet. Thanks.

Sam: It's so good to see you. I've been waiting all day.

Willa: I was just helping my mom start to unpack.

Sam: Can you play?

Willa: What?

Sam: I mean, can you stay? Outside for a while, I mean.

Willa: I don't think so. I'm just supposed to find the dweeb and bring him home.

Sam: Already? But you just got here.

Willa: Well, my grandma just got to our house, and she brought dinner.

Benji: Oh, good! What'd she bring? Do you know if she brought that strawberry-rhubarb pie?

Willa: I don't know! Why don't you go see for yourself, barf bag?

Benji: Okay. See you, Sam!

[BEN exits.]

Sam: Well, maybe after dinner then.

Willa: I don't know what's happening with all the unpacking yet. And I don't want my mom snooping in any of my stuff.

Sam: Oh, well, you must have a lot to do. Do you want some help?

Willa: No thanks. Maybe tomorrow, okay?

Sam: Sure. Tomorrow's fine. See you.

[WILLA *starts out. Turns around.*]

Willa: Sam? Thanks for the banner. It's really . . . adorable.
[*Exits.*]

Sam: You're welcome. You're welcome home.
[*Exits.*]

SCENE FIVE: WILLA'S DANCE STEPS

[WILLA *enters, listening to a Jann Arden song on her tape deck. Sam follows, carrying her whale puppet and her sewing basket.*]

Willa: Hi! . . . Don't you just love this song?

Sam: Sure, I guess.

Willa: Can you believe she's from Cowtown?

Sam: Of course!

Willa: When I said I was moving back to Calgary, all my Vancouver friends wondered if I'd get to see Jann Arden.

Sam: See her?

Willa: I said, "Sure, pas de problem. No problem."

Sam: At a concert, you mean?

Willa: More like at her house. I told them we could find out where she lives and just wait outside for her to come out.

Sam: And say what?

Willa: We could tell her we want to be in her next video.

Sam: Just like that.

Willa: Absolutely. We could tell her we're her biggest fans.

Sam: We are?

Willa: We could camp right on her curb. Wearing Jann Arden T-shirts. She'd have to notice us right?

Sam: I guess.

Willa: Hey, that's an awesome bracelet. Where'd you get it?

Sam: I made it. Got these at Beadworks.

Willa: No way.

Sam: Sure. I could show you.

Willa: Really? That'd be great. I've been working on a dance step to this song. Come on, I'll show you.

Sam: Well . . . I . . .

Willa: Come on. Put down your stuff. What is all this anyway?

Sam: It's my whale puppet. I wanted to show it to you. I was going to ask you to help me put it together.

Willa: Maybe later. Let's do this first.

[WILLA grabs the stuff and puts it aside. She turns on her music and starts to do the dance, trying unsuccessfully to get SAM to follow her.]

Willa: One, two, three, and turn. Okay, now you try.

Sam: I'm not so good at this.

Willa: It just takes practice.

Sam: But I don't . . .

Willa: You don't know this song?

Sam: No.

Willa: Don't you listen to the radio?

Sam: Not much. In the car, I guess, when we go on trips.

Willa: That is just so out of it.

Sam: No it's not. I'm just busy I guess.

Willa: With what?

Sam: Soccer. Swim club. You know, piano lessons, Girl Guides. Stuff like that.

Willa: You're still going to Girl Guides?

Sam: Yeah. Why?

Willa: It's for gumbies.

Sam: It is not. You used to love it.

Willa: Well, not anymore. My mom made me go when we first got to Vancouver. But me and my friend Sydney? We used to skip out and go to the mall.

Sam: To do what?

Willa: To hang! Just to hang, you know. What else?

Sam: What about swim club? Aren't you gonna want to come back?

Willa: Maybe. But not until I lose five pounds. I'm not letting anybody see me in a bathing suit. I look like a tubbo.

Sam: No, you don't. I mean. Who cares? . . .

Willa: If we're going to be dancers in Jann Arden's next video, we have to be really skinny. Like Claudia Schiffer.

Sam: Like who?

Willa: Are you serious? She's only, like, the most famous supermodel of the world.

Sam: Oh. Well, I knew that.

Willa: Don't you read magazines?

Sam: Yes.

Willa: What's your favorite?

Sam: I don't know. *National Geographic,* I guess.

Willa: Girlfriend . . . you need help. Looks like I got back here just in time.

Sam: In time for—

Willa: To bring you into the nineties!

Sam: What's wrong with *National Geographic?*

Willa: Nothing . . . except it's for geeks. Look after the tape player. I know just what you need. Wait right here.

Sam: Geeks?

[WILLA *exits.* SAM *gingerly approaches the tape player and turns the song back on. She slowly begins to dance. She circles around, not like* WILLA, *but in her own dreamy way. She is smiling.]*

SCENE SIX: WHALE WATCHING

[BEN *enters and notices the whale cut-out.]*

Ben: Cool.

Sam: Oh. Uh, thanks.

Ben: Did you make it?

Sam: Yeah, with a little help.

Ben: They're pretty small.

Sam: I know.

Ben: I mean, real whales? They're mondo huge!

Sam: I guess you saw some. When you lived in Vancouver?

Ben: You bet.

Sam: What was it like?

Ben: Well, the first ones we saw were at the aquarium. That was sort of . . .

Sam: Sad?

Ben: Yeah, I guess that's it.

Sam: I think it must be gross to see them all penned up like that.

Ben: Yeah, it's weird.

Sam: I'd rather I'd never see one than see them like that. I'd rather . . .

Ben: Rather what?

Sam: Save them.

Ben: You mean, rescue them.

Sam: Yeah.

Ben: Like *Rescue 911*.

Sam: Exactly.

Ben: It would be great to sneak in one night.

Sam: Unlock all the underwater doors.

Ben: And set them loose. Just like in *Free Willy!*

Sam: I love that movie.

Ben: Me, too.

Sam: They just went for it, right?

Ben: Getting it on the truck. That was my favorite part.

Sam: Going down that hill.

Ben: Through that car wash.

Sam: Across the beach.

Ben: Over the rocks.

Sam: Out to the open sea.

Ben: Out there . . . You just can't believe it. You know?

Sam: What?

Ben: You can see for miles.

Sam: Really?

Ben: You bet. You can see for . . . well, forever out there, Sam.

Sam: Must be great.

Ben: It's so big.

Sam: Did you get out there lots of times? On a boat, I mean.

Ben: Not as much as we'd like. I guess Willa told you about that whale watching trip?

Sam: No way! Did you really?

Ben: It was for a whole day. Figured Willa would have told you.

Sam: No.

Ben: Since you're so in love with whales.

Sam: She must have forgot.

Ben: Oh, too bad.

Sam: Well?

Ben: Well what?

Sam: Tell me.

Ben: Tell you what?

Sam: About the trip.

Ben: Oh, I dunno.

Sam: Why not?

Ben: What do I get?

Sam: I'll show you all the whale stuff I've got at home.

Ben: Like what?

Sam: I've got a mobile, a calendar. I've got one of those Japanese lanterns, you know? When you turn it on, the bulb heats up and makes the pictures turn. So it looks like the whales are dancing in a circle.

[Pause as SAM remembers this.]

When my mom gave it to me, do you know what she did?

Ben: What?

Sam: She made up this whole story about a little whale named Sophie that got separated from its family. There was this whole adventure part to it.

Ben: What do you mean?

Sam: Well, it was a little light show, a surprise for my birthday. She used the whole house to tell me this story. My mom's boyfriend, Geoff, helped her. We started in the basement with a flashlight, and she gave me a little stuffed whale. It was Sophie. She said Sophie had somehow become lost. And that's when Geoff put on the tape upstairs. You could hear the whale sounds fill the whole house!

    And my mom said that was the sound of the family of orcas who were coming to guide Sophie home.

    So we followed the whale sounds up to the main floor. That's when I saw they had strung little blue whale lights all the way up the stairs. More stuff happened, and then at the end of the story, she brought me up to my room at the very top of our house. Everything was dark except for . . .

Ben: Except for what?

Sam: Except for this little Japanese lantern with all the little whales dancing around in a circle. She told me that however far away from home Sophie or I got, the lights would always be on. That we should never be afraid to come home.

Ben: Can I play with it?

Sam: Sure. You have to be careful though. It's just made of rice paper.

Ben: No problem. I love paper stuff.

Sam: And on the way up to my room, I have a mural that covers the whole wall. Geoff painted it. It has one mother whale and a little one swimming beside her. He says it reminds him of us.

Ben: He sounds cool.

Sam: He's okay. I didn't like him at first.

Ben: Why not?

Sam: I dunno. Just used to it being my mom and me I guess. I liked it when he did the mural though. It's just me and my mom. He never tried to paint himself in or anything. Now will you just tell me?

Ben: Okay. We were out on this boat. We went for a whole day. Up to Robson Byte. We were out there for hours and hours. It was really cold, and I was so-o-o-o-o-o hungry. All there was to eat was Cheez Whiz sandwiches and lemonade. My socks were soaked. All I could think about was a hamburger, fries, and my nice warm *Star Trek* slippers.

And there was a little kid named Josie who just kept on whining and crying, "I wanna go home. I wanna go home." Everyone was about ready to do that, and they started to turn the boat around. Until Willa said, "Look, over there!" And everyone crowded over to where she was standing. At first, we thought it was just one.

Sam: But there were more?

Ben: Yeah. You could see one sort of rise out of the water. And then another. And another. There were about seven or eight of them. We all just stood and watched.

Sam: How big were they?

Ben: Beyond huge. Anything that big, you know? You just expect it to be awkward, clumsy. But they were so . . .

Sam: Graceful?

Ben: Exactly. Graceful. That's it. It was magic. Our little boat suddenly felt so small, like one of those Fisher Price boats in the bathtub. Everyone on the boat got real quiet. Even that little whiner, Josie. I forgot all about my wet feet.

[Quiet onstage as BEN remembers all this.]

Ben: Hey, we've got some photos of that trip. You want to see them?

Sam: Sure!

Ben: Okay. I'll go see if I can find them.

[BEN exits. Whale sounds up. SAM is alone onstage.]

SCENE SEVEN: TEEN MAGAZINES

[WILLA enters with a stack of teen magazines and a folder. The folder is a large cardboard art folder with the words Keep Out. Private. Hands Off. *written on the cover with red felt markers.*

Willa: Okay. Time to bring you into the 1990s.

Sam: What have you got?

Willa: *Sixteen, Young Miss.* And my favorite, *Big Bopper.*

Sam: Why is it your favorite?

Willa: Because of the center picture. See? You unfold the centre picture and you get a poster.

Sam: Oh, right.

Willa: See? I've got Jonathan Brandeis from *Seaquest.* And one of Jonathan Taylor Thomas. I brought over the best ones to show you.

Sam: Are they all called Jonathan?

Willa: What?

Sam: The guys? Never mind. What are you going to do with all these?

Willa: Put them up in my new room. My mom says I can decorate it however I like.

Sam: My mom let me do mine, too. I can show you.

Willa: Sure! I think she just wants to make it so I won't miss Vancouver.

Sam: But you're home now. Aren't you glad to be back?

Willa: Sort of, I guess. But I made tons-o-friends in Vancouver, you know. We did everything together.

Sam: Like what?

Willa: We'd plan what we were going to wear. Like on a Friday or something, we'd all wear green. Or on a Tuesday, we'd put on headbands. Earrings in our right ears only. Stuff like that.

Sam: Why?

Willa: So you could tell who was in and who was out. That's why.

Sam: In or out of what?

Willa: Our group, stupid.

Sam: Wouldn't you just know?

Willa: Know what?

Sam: Wouldn't you just know if they were in your group? Without having to dress the same?

Willa: Duh! Of course we'd know. We weren't doing it for us. We were doing it for the other girls. You know. The ones who wanted to be us.

Sam: You mean, you had sort of like a club? Like the one we used to have?

Willa: Clubs were okay when we were little. When it was okay to stick out like goofs. Now that's the last thing you want, right?

Sam: I guess.

Willa: Don't worry. I'm going to help you.

[WILLA excitedly opens the string on the art folder.]

Sam: What are these for?

Willa: These are the best. I wanna cover one whole wall in

autographed pictures and posters like this. I've been saving the ones I want to use the most. See? I've been keeping them in this special folder so they wouldn't get wrecked in the move. Here.

[WILLA carefully goes through the posters and selects one for SAM. She presents it to her proudly.]

Sam: What's this?

Willa: For you.

Sam: I don't really need anything for my room.

Willa: But I want you to have it. It's a present. A poster of The Cranberries.

Sam: Okay. Thanks.

Willa: What have you got? On your walls, I mean.

Sam: Well, it's mostly. . . nothing much, I guess. Some animal stuff I guess. Some lights. Junk like that.

Willa: Looks like I got here just in time to transform you. I know! I just got my allowance. Let's go to 7-Eleven.

Sam: For Slurpees ?

Willa: For *Teen Magic!* The new issue just came out, and it's got Jason Priestley on the cover.

Sam: Who's . . .

Willa: Come on. We can get Slurpees, too!

[They run out. Music up.]

SCENE EIGHT: PAPER AIRPLANES

[BEN enters.]

Ben: Sam? You out here? Sorry, but I can't find the pictures. Mom says we haven't got to the box with the albums yet. I'll get 'em for you later, though. *[sees pile of magazine pages]* Great! You found some paper! These are perfecto blecto. *[gets down and starts making paper airplanes out of WILLA's favorite magazine posters]* This paper is so nice and smooth.

[He folds up a few that aren't quite right, crumples them up, and starts over. During the following speech, he starts flying them around.]

And yes, ladies and germs, it's time to welcome you to the 1995 Annual Air Show. Right here on the edge of those dangerous Rocky Mountains. Right here in Calgary, Alberta, Canada. *[more building, more crashing, more crumpling of WILLA's treasured magazine posters]* It's true. It's the day you've all been waiting for! Benjamin Barnes is flying today. He is the youngest pilot in the daredevil group. Look at him take that spin. He'll take on any foe. No wonder they call him Fearless! It's true that he's been flying since he was nine years old. Just like you, he, too, needed a barf bag at one time. But not anymore!

[WILLA and SAM enter and see immediately what has happened. BEN does not see them at first and just continues playing.]

He has nerves of steel! Muscles of steel!

Willa: Brains of steel!

Ben: Oh, hi. Very funny.

Willa: What do you think you're doing?

Ben: I was just—

Willa: You took my posters.

Ben: I made some airplanes, that's all.

Willa: You used the posters I was saving for my room.

Ben: Sorry. I didn't—

Willa: What's all this?

Ben: Sam said she likes paper airplanes. I wanted to show her—

Willa: Don't be so stupid. She was probably just being polite or something.

Ben: But she—

Willa: She doesn't want to play paper airplanes with you. Do you, Sam?

Sam: Well, I . . .

Willa: We haven't played with this stuff since we were about four. Have we, Sam?

Sam: No.

Willa: Do you know why, you little moron?

[WILLA starts to crumple up all the paper airplanes that BEN has made. SAM wants to be as grown up as WILLA and joins her in the crumpling of the airplanes after a minute.]

Ben: Why?

Willa: Because we're not babies anymore, that's why. And paper airplanes are—

Sam: For babies. That's why.

Ben: *[to SAM]* But I thought you got us this paper and—

Sam: Why would I?

Ben: You said you wanted to see how to build a big plane.

Sam: Willa's right. I was just being . . .

Willa: Polite. Unlike you!

Ben: I'm sorry.

Willa: You wrecked everything. I've been saving those magazine posters for six months.

Ben: Sorry for living! I didn't know.

Willa: You don't know anything. That's your problem!

[WILLA and SAM start to leave. BEN follows them out.]

Ben: I'll get you some more.

Willa: Just get lost.

Ben: I'll use my allowance.

Willa: Just get lost. Hey, Sam, aren't you glad you don't have a little brother?

Sam: Yeah, I'm really glad about that.

[WILLA and SAM exit. BEN is alone onstage. Music up as

he crumples some more paper angrily. He is frustrated and suddenly lonely. He exits slowly.]

SCENE NINE: CROSSING FROM PLAYTIME

[Music up with a long enough cue to make it clear this is a different day. WILLA and SAM enter. WILLA carries two shopping bags of stuff. SAM carries a notebook and pen.]

Willa: Come on! I know if you just get started, you'll like it.

Sam: But I don't know what to say.

Willa: Well, get over it! Just say, "This is my very first fan letter. My friend Willa has written dozens of them. . . ."

Sam: Willa!

Willa: "But I was too busy playing with my trolls."

Sam: I was not. . . .

Willa: Just kidding!

Sam: I don't really want to do this.

Willa: How are you supposed to start an autographed picture collection unless you write some letters? I'm going to write about five more this afternoon.

Sam: I dunno.

Willa: We have to get you some decent pictures for your room. Once we get rid of more of this baby stuff.

Sam: We just painted it my favorite blue. Don't you like it?

Willa: Sure. The blue's okay. But how are you supposed to start thinking about clothes and looking cool and everything when all you've got is . . . *[holds up a backpack shaped like a teddy bear]* stuff like this?

Sam: I don't know.

Willa: All of this has got to go.

Sam: My Auntie Mary gave me that. For when I started Grade One.

Willa: Exactly. It's outta here.

Sam: *[pulls out some plastic jewelry]* Hey, can you believe I used to wear this stuff? And look at this! Trash or what?!
[SAM holds up a wrecked Barbie, then tosses it back into the bag. WILLA pulls out a stuffed whale.]

Willa: So is this. Definitely headed for the garbage.

Sam: It's only a little rip. I can sew that up and she'll be as good as new.

Willa: She's disgusting. Looks like a dog or somebody chewed her all up.

Sam: She's led a life of adventure!
[They both giggle.]

Willa: *[pulls out some old hats]* And look at all this dress-up stuff.

Sam: Those are the hats we used to wear when we played Aurora and Filomena.
[Music up as SAM takes one hat and grandly sweeps it on.]
Lady Filomena, at your service.
[SAM takes the other hat and offers it to WILLA in a formal way.]

Willa: Lady Aurora, accepting her wardrobe.
[WILLA accepts the hat. She puts it on, remembering.]

Sam: Are you ready for the story?
[The girls pause, look at each other.]
There once were two princesses. Named Aurora . . .

Willa: And Filomena.

Sam: Who were fearless. Heroic.

Willa: And strong. They both had golden hair.

Sam: Down to their knees.

Willa: And rode horses whenever they wanted.

Sam: For breakfast every day they ate . . .

Willa: Chocolate.

Sam: And grapes. After breakfast they would say . . .

Willa: Lady Aurora, are you ready?

Sam: Yes, Lady Filomena, I am ready.

> *[Over the next sequence, the girls remember the words to their old chant from those not-so-long-ago days when it was okay to pretend. They re-create the journey they used to take every time they played this game. The picnic table becomes the mountain, the cave, the valley as the memory and spirit of that enchanted time overtakes them.]*

Willa: Over the mountain to the valley of light.

Sam: Through the canyon of sand and wishes.

Willa: Silently moving past castle and hill.

Sam: Silently moving through shadows of caves.

Willa: Holding the vision of our very own place.

Sam: Holding the vision of sisters united.

Willa: Holding the vision of future enchantments.

Sam: We enter the magic realm of time.

Willa: We enter the magic realm of time

Both: We enter the magic realm of time.

> *[WILLA takes off the hat and slowly puts it back into the bag.]*

Willa: It used to be fun. Didn't it?

Sam: It sure was. The most fun I ever had.

Willa: We played that story every summer.

> *[WILLA takes off SAM's hat and puts it back into the bag.]*
> You still like to make up stories?

Sam: Sure.

Willa: You said you couldn't think of anything to put in the fan letter. Why don't you just make up a story?

Sam: I dunno.

Willa: You still like to play them, don't you?

Sam: What do you mean?

Willa: You still like to pretend them, play them out.

Sam: Sure . . . well, not really . . . I mean I guess I just sort of play them in my head, sometimes.

Willa: You sure you want me to throw all this stuff out?

Sam: Yeah.

Willa: Okay. I'll take it over now.

[SAM reaches in and takes out the stuffed whale. WILLA exits with the bags. SAM is alone clutching the whale. Music up.]

SCENE TEN: BEN'S TRUTH ABOUT VANCOUVER

[SAM sits alone with the stuffed whale. She puts it down gently on the table and crosses to the garage, where she has left the sewing basket used earlier for the puppet. She intends to repair the whale.

Ben enters before she has crossed back to the table. He sees the whale, takes it, and playfully tosses it in the air.]

Sam: Give that back.

Ben: Why should I?

Sam: Because it's mine.

Ben: Maybe not.

Sam: Why?

Ben: Maybe stuffed animals are for babies.

Sam: Benji . . .

Ben: Just like paper airplanes are for babies.

Sam: Stop it.

Ben: No, you stop it. You said you were going to show me all your stuff. You promised.

Sam: I know. But Willa wants to . . .

[At the mention of WILLA, BEN's teasing becomes less playful. His anger at being excluded earlier comes out.]

Ben: Who cares what Willa wants?

Sam: I do.

Ben: Why?

Sam: Because she's my best friend, that's why.

Ben: No she's not. She thinks you're a baby.

Sam: What are you talking about?

> [SAM *grabs at the stuffed whale. They are both grabbing and pulling at it over the next few lines. As they yank at the whale, the foam stuffing inside starts to fall out in large chunks.*]

Ben: In Vancouver? She made fun of all your letters. Remember when you wrote her the blub-blub language?

Sam: Yeah. But how? . . .

Ben: Or signed them with that Filomena stuff you used to play?

Sam: How did you know? . . .

Ben: She'd bring your letters to school and make fun of them to her new friends.

Sam: No way.

Ben: Yes way. She laughed at them.

Sam: She wouldn't do that.

Ben: You taped some letters to her, right?

Sam: That's right.

Ben: Willa used to play them for her friends, and they'd make fun of you.

Sam: No way.

Ben: Yes way. You wanna know what they called you?

Sam: Benji . . .

Ben: You wanna know? You wanna know?

> [*The stuffed whale comes apart in* BEN'S *hands.*]

Sam: Sophie . . .

Ben: I'm . . . Maybe I can fix . . .

> [BEN *tries to give* SAM *back the whale. She shakes her head.*]

Sam: Just tell me what they'd say.

Ben: Forget it.

Sam: Tell me. Just tell me right now.

Ben: Okay! They'd call you Sucky Sam. They'd say let's hear the "whale-head." Play the "loser part" again.

[SAM is unable to say anything. She sits quietly.]

Sam: But Willa wouldn't do that. . . .

Ben: Yes, she would. They'd rewind and laugh.

Sam: But Willa's my best friend. She wouldn't.

[WILLA enters, running. She has not heard any of this.]

Ben: Well she did. Why don't you just ask her? She's right behind you.

[BEN exits, still carrying the whale.]

SCENE ELEVEN: WILLA'S DEFENSE

Willa: Ask me what?

Sam: Nothing.

Willa: You can ask me anything.

Sam: Okay. What about Vancouver?

Willa: What about it?

Sam: What was it like? Living there, I mean?

Willa: It's fun. Everyone is so cool. All their clothes and everything. You can go to the beach every day if you want.

Sam: That must be great.

Willa: It is. There's so much to do. Cowtown is just so . . .

Sam: So what?

Willa: So boring.

Sam: What about friends? Did you make a lot of friends while you were there?

Willa: Oh, sure. I was really popular.

Sam: What are their names?

Willa: There's Jackie. She's got Docs in about ten different colors. Then there's Marianne. She has three earrings on one ear and two on the other. Let's see. Courtenay. She just got her very own CD player.

Sam: Did you have a best friend?

Willa: You mean, like you and I used to call each other?

Sam: Exactly.

Willa: Well, no. Because I think "best friends" are sort of . . .

Sam: Sort of what?

Willa: Well, sort of wimpy, I guess.

Sam: Just as wimpy as keeping promises? Like when we promised to write every day. Remember that?

Willa: Yeah. I . . .

Sam: But after a few months, you hardly wrote at all.

Willa: Yes, I did. I . . .

Sam: I thought I just needed to try harder. So I wrote letters. Taped letters. Sometimes I'd send two in one day.

Willa: Sam, I . . .

Sam: I missed you so much.

Willa: I missed you, too.

Sam: You hardly ever wrote back. I figured you must be busy.

Willa: I was!

Sam: Oh, yeah? Busy laughing at me with your new friends?

Willa: No. I mean . . .

Sam: How could you laugh at my letters, Willa?

Willa: What?

Sam: You and your Vancouver friends. Courtenay and Jackie and Marianne.

Willa: But how did . . . I mean . . . did Benji?

Sam: He told me all about it. He said you called me Sucky Sam.

Willa: We were just . . .

Sam: Just tell me one thing, Willa.

Willa: Okay, I . . .

Sam: Is it true or not? True or not.

Willa: Yeah, but . . . it was the only way to get them to stop.

Sam: By letting them call me names. Like loser? Whale-head? Sucky Sam?

Willa: Please, just listen to me.

Sam: Why should I?

Willa: Because you don't get it.

Sam: Get what?

Willa: What it's like to move! It's awful. You never had to do it. You never just got stuck in a new place. Where you had no friends. When I got there, I found out one thing, okay? Nobody has time for a new kid in the summer. The only person I had to play with was Benji. And even he didn't have time for me.

Sam: What's all this got to do with calling me names?

Willa: Just listen, okay? Will you just listen, please? There was this one red-haired girl at the end of our block. I used to see her go off on her bike. I used to sit on the ledge out in the front of our house, wishing she'd see me. You know, stop and say hi. I sat there every day for weeks. I even sat out there when it rained. Got soaked. Didn't matter. She just rode right past me. That was my summer. Welcome to Vancouver, right? Couldn't wait until the first day of school. My mom got me new black overalls from The Gap. And I was wearing my hair in two braids. You know with those little beaded things on the ends, like I used to wear it. It was a big school, way bigger than Sunnyside. I was trying so hard to be brave. You know . . . Aurora the fearless and all that.

Had to stand up, say my name, where I was from. That was pretty gross, but when I sat down again, I remember I took a deep breath and started to feel okay about stuff. It was the first time I felt like I had a chance.

I was finally in a place where I could make some friends.
Then I heard it for the first time. Hick.

Hick—Hiccup . . . I thought it was some sort of a joke. I was smiling. You now, when I turned around. There were four girls, and they were all laughing. Took me a couple of minutes before I . . . before I got that they were laughing at me.

Sam: Why?

Willa: Because they decided I was a hick. Because I wore braids. Because I was from Cowtown, because I wasn't like them. They all had short hair. They're into using gel, stuff like that. And they think clothes from The Gap are out of it. I kept hearing that word *hick* over and over.

Sam: What did you do?

Willa: I wanted to sink into my desk. To disappear. Never thought that afternoon would end. When I got home, I told my mom I was sick. Worked for one day. Stayed in my room and tried to figure out how to get out of going to school. For the rest of my life. Had to go back the next day. I came down the hall, and they saw me. I heard it start. *Hiccup, hiccup.* "I feel the hiccups coming on," or "Wish I could get rid of these hiccups."

Sam: Couldn't you go one of the teachers?

Willa: Never happened when they were around. They did it mostly before school, out on the steps. At lunchtime, stuff like that. They'd make it sound like a game or something. Everyone started doing it.

Stopped wearing braids. Cut my hair. Got my mom to buy me some Club Monaco sweatshirts because that's what they all wore. It was too late though. I listened to them hiccup for three months.

Then one day we were talking about whales in class. Don't know why, but I got my nerve up and told them I

had a friend back home who was really into whales.
And Marianne said, "You mean she's a whale-head?" And
I said, "Guess so." And they said you sounded sucky.

Sam: And what did you say?

Willa: You've got to understand. It was the first time they
ever talked to me! So I said . . . well I said you were. They
wanted to know more stuff. So I told them about your
microscope and your dinosaurs, the clubhouse . . .

Sam: You made fun of our clubhouse?

Willa: No, I didn't. But they were laughing, okay? And for the
first time, it wasn't at me. It felt so good! And they asked
me what your name was. When I said Sam, Jackie said,
"Sucky Sam." And everyone thought . . . hilarious, right?
So I laughed, too. And Marianne asked me to bring my
Sucky Sam letters to school. And suddenly, I knew they
liked me. Because they stopped calling me hick. They
just need somebody to bully. . . . Doesn't matter who.
It's like . . . all they wanna do is sit around and laugh at
somebody. That's what they do for fun . I guess because
it's more grown up or something.

Sam: And what's so grown up about teasing people?

Willa: I don't know. All I know is that's when they stopped
picking on me. . . .

Sam: And started picking on me.

Willa: But you weren't even there. It wasn't like you could
hear us! You were all the way across the Rocky Mountains.

Sam: Right. So I couldn't fight back.

Willa: But you didn't have to. You weren't even there.

Sam: No, I wasn't. But you were.

Willa: You don't get it. I was just trying . . .

Sam: You're the one that doesn't get it, Willa Barnes. You
never stood up for me.

Willa: No, I didn't. But nobody ever called you a hick to your face.

Sam: They called me names and you let them.

Willa: It's way worse when it's to your face. You don't know how much it hurts.

Sam: Yes, I do Willa. Maybe not before today. But I do now.

Willa: Sam . . . Sam!

[SAM takes a long look at WILLA and then walks out. WILLA is left alone onstage. She is confused and angry. Music up as she struggles with her feelings. WILLA exits.]

SCENE TWELVE: REDISCOVERING PLAYTIME

[Two days later. Music up. BEN enters. He's holding nothing. Doing nothing, saying nothing. He climbs up on the picnic table. Fools around with the clothesline. Sits down dejectedly.

WILLA enters, carrying a closed cardboard box. On top of the box is her pile of magazines.]

Willa: Hey, Ben.

Ben: Hey, Willa.

Willa: Whatcha doing?

Ben: Nothing.

Willa: What's the matter?

Ben: No one to play with.

Willa: How come?

Ben: Kevin's gone on holidays. Jeff's at camp. And now Dad says we can't go hiking till August.

Willa: Isn't there anyone else around?

Ben: Not my age.

Willa: Where'd you go after lunch?

Ben: I saw some bigger kids playing baseball at the park.

Willa: So you went over there?

Ben: Thought if I watched for a while, they'd ask me to play.

Willa: What happened?

Ben: Nothing. Just sat there on the bench with my glove.

Willa: And they never asked you to play?

Ben: Nope.

Willa: So they never noticed you at all?

Ben: Nope. It's like I was invisible.

Willa: Those jerks. How long did you wait?

Ben: All afternoon. Till I started to get this feeling in my stomach.

Willa: I know that one. Sort of cold. Rumbly.

Ben: Yeah. How did you know?

Willa: Big sisters are supposed to know stuff. Sometimes, anyway.

Ben: Oh.

Willa: What are you gonna do now?

Ben: Nothing. I'm just gonna sit here. For the rest of my life.

Willa: *[picks up one of her teen magazines]* Hey, Ben! Didn't you say this shiny paper makes the best planes?

Ben: Yeah, but I thought those were . . .

[WILLA slowly tears a page from one of the magazines. She begins to fold it.]

Willa: Forget it.

Ben: But I thought these were your private magazines.

Willa: I can always get more. Take some.

Ben: Thanks!

Willa: You know what you gotta understand about me, Ben?

Ben: What?

Willa: Sometimes I can be a jerk, too! *[makes a paper airplane and tries to fly it]* And now, taking off in her glider for today's race, it's flyer Willa Barnes, champion of the jerks. *[speaks as she flies it around the yard]*

Willa: Here comes the TV news team to ask her the question

of the day: "Miss Barnes, Miss Barnes . . . Why are you such a jerk?"

Ben: *[rolling up another magazine to make an imaginary microphone]* Come on, Miss Barnes. *Hard Copy* wants to know.

Willa: Trying to be cool, I guess.

Ben: Trying to be cool. Miss Barnes! Miss Barnes!

Willa: What is it? I am preparing for takeoff.

Ben: If you fold down these sides like this, you'll get a much better glide.

Willa: Thanks. But let's make a bigger one. Just a sec.

[WILLA runs off.]

Ben: *[looking offstage]* Hey, Sam. Come here. Look what we're doing.

[SAM enters.]

Ben: We're going to make a big glider.

[WILLA hurries in with her precious art folder of magazine posters.]

Willa: Hi.

Sam: Oh. Hi.

[BEN interrupts, eager to keep on playing.]

Ben: Is that the stuff you brought to use?

Willa: Yeah. You go ahead by yourself.

Ben: But I thought you were gonna play. . . .

Willa: Just wait a minute, Ben. You can fold up these posters and make some of those big gliders.

Ben: Neat!

Willa: Except J. T. T. That's Jonathan Taylor Thomas. Leave him alone, okay?

Ben: Jonathan Taylor Thomas. Got it.

[BEN takes the posters and sits away from the girls, folding his planes.]

Willa: Never saw you for a couple of days.

Sam: Been busy.

Willa: Ever since . . .

Sam: I know.

Willa: Look, Sam. I'm really sorry. I didn't think . . .

Sam: Yeah, well. . .

Willa: Ben and I were just talking about it.

Sam: About what?

Willa: About what a jerk I can be.

Ben: She's Queen of the Jerks! Most of the time.

Willa: I wanted to ask you something.

Sam: Well, ask me then.

Willa: Will you just . . . *[swallows the words, can't get them out]*

Sam: What?

Willa: Will you just give me another chance? To be friends, I mean? I never meant to hurt you. I never did.

Sam: Willa, I . . .

Willa: I know you probably won't want to be best friends again. But if you'll just try to . . .

Sam: I don't know if I can. . . .

Willa: I'll try harder. I'll try harder at everything, I promise. *[WILLA brings SAM the cardboard box. Opens it up.]*

Willa: Look, I brought this back. Climbed right into the dumpster to get it.

Sam: You did? *[pulls out the teddy bear backpack]*

Willa: Yeah. It's your stuff. You should be the one to decide how long you want to keep it. Not me.

Sam: Thanks.

Willa: *[pulls Sophie out of the box]* And I've been trying to fix . . .

Sam: Sophie.

Willa: Yeah. Benji told me what happened. I haven't finished it yet. Maybe we can do it together.

Sam: Okay.

Willa: Great. What are you doing? Right now, I mean?

Sam: Nothing.

Willa: I'm going to make up an adventure for my little brother. There's no one around for him. You know, to play with. I wanna cheer him up. So . . . can you stay? I mean, can you play?

Sam: Well, I . . .

Willa: We used to make up the best adventures! Don't you remember?

Sam: Sure I do.

Willa: We were the champions. Right?

Sam: Right!

[The girls connect for a minute.]

Willa: So you'll stay?

Sam: Okay.

Willa: Great!

Ben: Oh Filomena; oh Aurora. *[teasing them about getting mushy]* Mmmm, mmmm.

Sam and Willa: Benji!

Ben: Wait. Watch this.

[BEN throws paper airplane. SAM catches it and sends it flying.]

Sam: Hey! We could build our own plane!

[WILLA starts swinging boards and junk around, climbing up as high as they can get her.]

Willa: It's gotta be bigger than a glider.

Sam: A glider only holds one person.

Willa: I know! A hot air balloon!

Ben: A blimp!

Sam: A helicopter!

Willa: A jet!

Sam: Hey, Ben! How about a space shuttle!

Willa: Exactly!

[They start to build a plane, and they describe the process as they do it. As the construction is completed, the dialogue picks up.]

Willa: It'll be just like Apollo 13. Those astronauts were brave.

Sam: And fearless.

Ben: Going where no man . . .

Sam: Or woman!

Ben: . . . has gone before!

[Music. Chaos. Lots of sound and energy as they transform the boards, tires, all that stuff, into a spaceship. They are buckling in and pulling on imaginary headgear. It's completely wacko out there. Lots of music during the takeoff. They have climbed up as high as they can get. They are seated a la Star Trek. The takeoff is initially very bumpy and loud.]

Ben: The shuttle is ready to lift off, Captain.

Willa: Is the Sunnyside crew standing by?

Ben: Standing by, Captain.

Sam: Standing by, Captain.

Willa: We seem to be having some turbulence.

Ben: It's too late to stop! All the engines are fired.

Sam: They've started the countdown.

Willa: Hang on, people. We're in for a rocky blast-off!

Sam: Ten, nine, eight . . .

Ben: Did you make sure . . .

Sam: Six, five . . .

Ben: . . . all the doors were locked?

Willa: Four, three,

All: Two, one.

Willa: We are outta here!

[They somehow play out of their seats into slow motion. One of the boards they were using slowly

becomes a deck. They are all laying on the deck and peering over the edge. They need to be as high up as possible. They are looking down at the earth from a great distance. They each point things out.]

Captain's log. Summer 1995 . . .

Sam: Look, there's Africa!

Willa: Wow! And there's China!

Sam: There's the Pacific Ocean!

Ben: There's Vancouver!

Sam: There's my dad's place on Blackfish Sound.

Ben: Sam—a pod of whales—look!

[They're so busy watching the whales, they almost run into the Rockies.]

Willa: Look out! There's the Rocky Mountains!

Sam: There's Calgary! I can see the Calgary Tower!

Ben: Hey, there's Peter's Drive-In!

[Pause as they look around.]

Sam: It's great up here.

Ben: It's *big* up here.

Willa: The earth—it looks so little.

Sam: Everybody looks tiny. Like little Munchkins.

Ben: Look at them all hurry around.

Sam: They should just . . .

Willa: Slow down a little. Stop being in such a hurry all the time.

Sam: They might not know. . . .

Willa: Know what?

Sam: How big it is.

Willa: How they've got all this space.

Sam: To do whatever they want.

Willa: Right.

[In slow motion, they look around some more. Music comes up over these last few lines.]

Ben: Houston, we've got a problem,

Willa: What is it?

Ben: Did we remember to pack the barf bag?

[Lots of commotion, calamity, laughter as WILLA and SAM climb down, helping BEN down, then chasing him out.]

Sam: Oh, grosserama!

Ben: Gotcha, didn't I?

Willa: We brought you, didn't we? You are a barf bag!

[Music up.
Fin.]